TRAVELS WITH MY CHICKEN

TRAVELS
WITH MY
CHICKEN

A MAN AND HIS COMPANION
TAKE TO THE ROAD

Martin Gurdon

The Lyons Press
Guilford, Connecticut
An imprint of The Globe Pequot Press

Designed by Ian Hughes, Mousemat Design Ltd
Illustrations by Phil Garner

Library of Congress Cataloging-in-Publication Data

Gurdon, Martin.
    Travels with my chicken : a man and his companion take to the road / Martin
Gurdon.—1st Lyons Press ed.
        p. cm.
    ISBN 1-59228-778-6
    1. Great Britain—Description and travel. 2. Gurdon, Martin—Travel—Great
Britain. 3. Chickens—Great Britain—Anecdotes. I. Title.

DA632.G87 2005
914.104'86—dc22
                                                                    2005044963

ACKNOWLEDGMENTS

Thanks to Mic Cheetham, Kate Michell (the blue pencil is mightier than the sword—but a gun would be useful sometimes), Yvonne Thynne, and Catherine Holmes. Also, Sarah Crawford—and finally, George Collins, who didn't get mentioned in the last book. Sorry.

This one's for David, Jenny, and especially, Jane.

www.martin-gurdon.co.uk

Con

tents

Further Travels

Introduction

Have chicken, will travel. It's not an obvious idea for a book. It was arrived at more or less by accident—and, frankly, I didn't dream it up. That honor falls to literary agent Mic Cheetham.

Mic, who is one of nature's good people, looks after my book-writing endeavors: to wit, something on old cars, which nobody wanted, and a humor book with the self-explanatory title of *Hen and the Art of Chicken Maintenance*, which the publishers of this one, New Holland, liked and decided to go with.

I live in the countryside with a cat, a dog, some chickens, and, most significantly, a woman called Jane. As a child I'd been dispatched to live with an aunt and uncle in Lancashire after my mother became ill, and was allowed to keep a few hens in the far recesses of their garden. Jane, who, like me, originated from chicken-free Kew, Surrey, saw a certain romanticism in this activity. Having decided that she wanted to live with me, she realized that this would also involve sharing our lives with some hens. So it proved, and their activities (escapes, passion, death, power struggles, vast medical bills, and a sex change) were curiously engaging, and I ended up knocking out a book about them.

To promote it, I traveled across England from Tunbridge Wells to Aberystwyth, usually with only a hen for company, and eventually Mic started muttering about there being another book in our experiences. This is the result.

It starts with some events that preceded and overlapped those journeys and shaped how I looked at them, and there are a few caveats. This book should really be called *Travels with My Chickens*,

since more birds than one were involved, but, for practical and animal-husbandry reasons, I traveled with only one animal at a time. Sticking with the singular of the title just seemed to work better.

Also, there are one or two chronological sleights of hand to help the narrative along. This is cheating, but, unless you were one of the people Peeping Chicken, Tikka, Vera, and I met, and have a photographic memory, you'll never know.

Finally, names used in the chapter about visiting Ford Prison were changed for a variety of obvious reasons.

The end result is a book about people and places as much as it is about chickens, which, for the sake of my sanity and perhaps yours, is probably a good thing.

Part 1

Light
and
Shade

1

On the Box,
In the Box

R!SE AND SHINE!

We never met Tori Amos.

For those who don't know, Tori Amos is an American singer who does angst with a capital A—not an Amish homestead. While Tori was in the green room, we were shown to a sort of giant cupboard. It was dimly lit and drainpipe-sized cables wriggled across the floor. Two middle-aged men in overalls were hunched in a corner watching *R!se*, the Channel 4 breakfast TV show which seemed to be populated mainly by nubile lovelies in tiny vests.

As these visions of bubblegum pertness flittered across the screen, tea was slowly ingested by the two men, who watched the primary-colored comings and goings with the studied indifference of a pair of cats considering the contents of a goldfish bowl.

"Hello," I said, putting down the cat box containing the chicken.

Two heads nodded an acknowledgment, but the *R!se* nymphets continued to hold their owners' attentions.

There was a small irony to this slightly slack-jawed tableau, because about thirty feet away from us the BBC's alternative to the de-caffeinated zaniness we were watching was in full swing. Our little annex was part of the studio complex from which the BBC1 *Breakfast* program was broadcast. It was 8:45 on a dull November morning and I was there as a guest because I had written a book, *Hen and the Art of Chicken Maintenance*.

Promoting the book had briefly taken over my life. I seemed to be spending a lot of time going to unlikely places in the company of a live chicken, one of the small flock of birds who live at the bottom of our garden.

I'm a freelance journalist. Mostly I write about cars, but combine the words "freelance" and "journalist," and you have the definition of a serial opportunist. Basically, I'll write about anything, and a good bit of my work is inspired—if that's the word—from things that go on

around me. Many of the junker cars I've owned have more or less paid for themselves, thanks to the junker stories they've been used to illustrate. Before getting married, I'd even sold a story about the ghastliness of wedding-related magazines and the soft-focus hard sell they employ, although the newspaper that took the piece spiked it after landing a big reader promotion with a publisher of these things.

Jane, my wife, and I don't have children, but if we did, I'd doubtless find some way of exploiting the fact by writing about it. KIDDIES IN FIRST BOWEL MOVEMENT SHOCK would surely yield a thousand words, or perhaps a dimple-cheeked moppet displaying a special gift for toddler hang-gliding would help pay for the mortgage if a double-page spread could be wrung out of it. Well, maybe. No kids equals no checks, but, determined bastard that I am, an obvious alternative had suggested itself.

The interest our chickens generated had caused the journalistic antennae to twitch. I reasoned that if our birds made our friends laugh there might be a story to be had from this. The story turned into *Hen*.

So, now I was shamelessly hawking my wares and discovering that this was fun—certainly more fun than real life, which at the time seemed to be crowding in with a lot of bleak realities.

CHICKEN SCOOP

In itself, writing a book about chickens does not get you on television, and I had no illusions that the BBC had made the booking because they thought I was going to be a brilliant interviewee. Baggy automotive journalists who spend their spare time writing hen-related humor books are not the stuff of lifestyle TV. No, they had invited me because I had offered to bring a chicken. She was a Buff Sussex pullet—that is, a teenaged bird—called Peeping Chicken, a name chosen because her voice hadn't quite broken so she peeped rather than clucked. As a co-interviewee, she was likely to be

conversationally challenged, but, in terms of cuteness and strangeness, she would beat me hands—or claws—down.

We were lucky to be at the interview at all, however, as at the time Peeping and I were originally expected at the BBC's White City studios, we were sitting in the back of Britain's most weary Ford Galaxy minicab, grinding along the road, surrounded by other pissed-off, traffic-bound drivers.

I live in rural Kent, but to ease the stress (ha, ha) had come to London and stayed at my father and stepmother's house near Uxbridge, so as to be closer to the studio. On a good day the A40 is a ten-minute drive from their front door. This was not a good day.

"It's not usually like this," said the minicab driver. A nice man with an anxious pear-shaped face, he had a problem with maps, which in career terms was surely a serious demerit. The only reason we were in the Devil's traffic jam was because we were already running late. Why? Because this guy had misread his map en route to collect us and had gone to the wrong street. He was slightly late arriving there and phoned to ask where our house was. We told him it was about five miles away.

He seemed inclined to argue about this, but after some slightly frantic persuading navigated his way to a neighboring street. Then he phoned and insisted that the road of 1930s homes where my folks live was not marked on any map. We insisted that it was, and by a small fluke he finally appeared, only twenty minutes late.

Not entirely trusting his sense of place, I asked what route he planned to take to the BBC in Shepherd's Bush. It was pretty much forty-five degrees in the wrong direction, so, feeling only mildly hysterical, I suggested an alternative, picked up his map and discovered that several pages were missing. This explained a lot.

His car had that minicab patina: threadbare seats topped off with a thin fuzz of synthetic purple butt lint, teased from their weave by

being sat on twenty-three hours a day for most of the past half-decade. The dark-blue door trims were a mix of plastic, scratches, and lightly polished dirt. An off-yellow warning light glowed dimly behind the dust that covered the instrument panel. Electric window switches rocked like loose milk teeth, and the car's interior was imbued with that late-night smell of cigarette smoke and fried food. Chemically unnatural "pine" air freshener that would suffocate the most determined horsefly and neutralize the smell of a drunk's vomit mingled with other people's aftershave and sweat. Now the stench of chicken shit was joyfully mating with these odors to create a new super-smell that could rot flesh and unravel man-made fibers.

I opened a window and breathed in damp air and traffic fumes.

As we ground slowly forward the driver said almost nothing. Occasionally he would shake his head sadly and mutter, "Oh, dear!" or "Oh, God!" You can imagine how soothing that was.

I'd put an outdoor coat over Peeping Chicken's travel box, which was perched on the seat beside me. The idea was to prevent her being freaked out by the slowly moving herd of traffic. I could hear the

occasional scrabbling noise as she rooted about for something to eat. At least one of us wasn't worried.

We made it. It seemed as if enough slack had been built into our journey time to have just about allowed for a major detour, but an extra fifteen minutes' delay would have mucked everything up, and I found myself shaking the driver's hand rather than his throat.

FOWL PLAY

Getting to the studio had been a trial, but getting a chicken on television at all had not been a simple process either. How had this been achieved? The shameful truth is that I'd asked.

"Er, please can I come on TV and plug my book?"

Thousands of books emerge every year, and most of them vanish without a trace. I'd recently met a published novelist who was also a bookshop manager. He said that, in the unlikely event of getting into print in the first place, an unknown author might make about $1,400 and see a thousand copies produced. That's a pretty small return for years of graft, and it's easy to see why the "we'll-publish-your-book" merchants can afford to advertise in the national press.

Although there are many obvious exceptions. If you're an author, being young, telegenic, well connected, famous, or a newspaper columnist are all means of getting your book noticed, reviewed, and generally publicized. Authoring something that fits into an easily recognized genre helps, too.

So, I was starting out with several strikes against me. I was aging, obscure, and, frankly, pretty well disconnected, and had written a comic magnum opus about domestic fowl. Surely this was going to appeal only to bird lovers with dung-encrusted boots, wasn't it? If this constituency was interested, then I was more than delighted—but getting the idea across that the book had been written for people who actually didn't know or care about the subject had needed a certain

amount of persistence and a lot of brass balls. It came as a surprise to discover just how much brass balls I had.

A little detective work identified the producer of *Breakfast*. I cobbled together a begging e-mail, along with a press release, but before sending the thing I wondered how to make it stand out a bit. Then inspiration struck. My dad had passed on an e-mail comprising a basic but funny cartoon of a big band whose members were all chickens. They were playing a synthesized version of "In the Mood," but, to give the whole thing a real touch of class, the tune was clucked. The creator of this musical delight was French and presumably had nothing better to do, but it suited my purposes, and this was cut and pasted onto the "give us an interview" missive.

So, when my quarry opened the e-mail he had a quick blast of "In the Mood" sung by chickens, which got his attention, and meant that he did at least read the cover letter, offering two guests in human and bird form. Instead of hitting the delete key he passed on my stuff to one of the program's bookers. She got in touch and asked to see copies of *Hen* and, to my great surprise, an invitation duly arrived.

As this was the BBC, Peeping was the subject of a risk-management assessment form, and my contact sent several slightly apologetic e-mails covering a gamut of televisual disasters that could overtake a Buff Sussex hen.

Would the hen be in a box? There seemed to be some concern that I'd emerge from a minicab with the bird tucked under my arm. What would happen if she escaped and pecked the assistant lighting director to death? What if the camera operator had some terrible avian allergy if s/he was within ten paces of a free-range hen? What would be the result of Peeping's defecating on the charming but frighteningly clean-looking Natasha Kaplinsky, one of the program's hosts? Would there be a payout to Tori Amos if Peeping pecked her index finger, ruining her ability to play the piano?

These, or similar, things had to be considered before Peeping and I were allowed on the premises, and, when we were, there had presumably been some sort of executive health-and-safety confab, which meant that we were dispatched to the hole in the wall with the tea-drinking *R!se* lovers and the big cables, rather than the room where interviewees sat around before spending three minutes or so talking about their books/films/plays/documentaries/stuff.

Not that I was complaining. Now that I'd gotten this far, the whole experience had a slightly surreal edge to it and was hugely entertaining. Post-minicab, part of my critical facilities had detached themselves from the event itself, so it was possible to watch what was going on from a standpoint where the incipient sense of terror that bubbled away somewhere near the thinking bit of my subconscious never quite subsumed it, like ink in blotting paper. My brain seemed to be functioning quite well.

So did Peeping Chicken. She sat in her cat box with the openable, "cabriolet" lid, pecking intermittently at the contents of the margarine container that was now stuffed with wild birdseed. It was pretty dark, but that didn't stop her from attacking the food with enthusiasm.

I found a sink and topped off Peeping's water container. Then a woman strode into the room, advanced purposefully toward me, and clapped a couple of pink powder-puff objects to my ears. This apparently meant that I was now made up.

Peeping and I had about five minutes to go before we were on. I studied the room looking for obstacles over which I could trip or containers with liquid that I might spill over myself. Coordination is not one of my strengths and, although things have improved a bit since adolescence—when I'd walk on my own foot and swear loudly, or casually shut one of my hands in a car window—a capacity to upend objects (especially when I'm tired, tense, or stressed) has remained.

Anyway, back to the BBC. Although mentally I didn't feel especially twitchy, I knew that every nerve ending and sinew would conspire against me, given the chance.

CAMERA! ACTION!

I had visions of tripping over a cable and doing a windmilling run-in to the middle of the studio, landing in a flapping heap on the floor and watching helplessly as an extruded-plastic cat box and its feathered cargo sailed missile-like toward a sofa-bound victim, then hearing a loud *crack!* as it connected with co-presenter Dermot Murnaghan's skull.

Instead, a young woman with a clipboard appeared and, clasping Peeping's portable prison, I followed her into the studio, making it to one of the plastic chairs behind the set, cameras, and crew without falling over anything.

It's odd the things you remember. It occurred to me that my chair was cold and rocklike, and that the studio, which on screen looked cavernous, was actually rather small. This was a little fake room set up in a space the size of an aircraft hangar, and where it stopped the *Newsnight* studio began. That, too, looked tiny and cluttered. The curving desks behind which the news anchors sat and shouted at important public figures were all shunted into a corner.

There weren't many people around. A small selection of clipboard carriers looked busy and slightly glamorous, and a young woman with headphones seemed to be overseeing the cameras trained on the two presenters, their guests, the figure-of-eight desk, and half-moon sofa.

Despite the pre-chilled chairs that would surely have made the most lugubrious hemorrhoid vibrate with glee, the place had a curiously intimate air, as if the people in it were having private conversations. This was good. Perhaps it would be possible to pretend that

the next few minutes of my life weren't going to be watched by 0.9 million adults who'd recently offloaded their school-aged children with a glad cry and flopped in front of their televisions for a bit of light relief.

A man in an elegant gray suit was sitting next to me. This was Charles Wheeler, the octogenarian ex-*Newsnight*, ex-*Panorama* journalist. It was the latter program's fiftieth birthday and he was going to talk about it. Wheeler's face had the profile of a bird of prey, and he radiated a natural gravitas. His expression was almost impassive as his eyes swiveled down to the cat box and its chunky occupant. Peeping rifled about in her bedding and ignored him.

What was Charles Wheeler thinking? Something along the lines of "Why on earth am I sitting next to a man with a chicken?" per-

haps? With a hint of stately bemusement he continued studying the cat box and said nothing. I muttered about having heard a radio series he'd made on British children sent to Australia as orphans during the 1950s, and how interesting it had been.

"Yes," said Charles Wheeler. "It was interesting to make." Peeping Chicken continued to hold his attention.

It was now 9 A.M. and the program had switched to a news bulletin and the young woman with the clipboard was back.

Charles Wheeler was ushered to one side of the large red sofa. I went to the other. He sat next to Dermot Murnaghan; I was directed to Natasha Kaplinsky. I plonked the cat box between us and shook hands with everybody. Both presenters were easygoing and appeared to be working hard at suppressing the urge to smile. Chicken-interviewing had probably not been part of either's career plans.

With a couple of minutes to go Natasha Kaplinsky asked sweetly if the chicken could sit on her lap. Until this point I'd continued to feel suffused with that odd sense of calm, but the question caused my guts to tighten unpleasantly.

I didn't say no, but burbled on about the potential effect of Peeping's digestive tract on the presenter's casually expensive clothes.

"You don't need to worry about that," she said, grinning hugely. "The director's promised to pay the dry-cleaning bill."

Damn! I thought. The real reason for my reluctance was that I'd no idea how much experience of hen-handling this elegant, polished person had. If Peeping escaped and hurled herself across the studio in a blizzard of feathers, perhaps leaving a lovely wet calling card on the desk, then skittered around the studio, loudly vocalizing her distress, would I have to go and rescue her mid-interview? If she refused to be caught I could see prolonged embarrassment resulting.

"Perhaps," I said, "she could sit on my lap to start with, and we'll see how we all get on—she's a bit nervous."

13

This seemed to satisfy my interrogator. Peeping was lifted out of her travel box, deposited on my lap, and offered a handful of grain, which she eyed but didn't touch.

"For most of us, chicken maintenance means deciding whether to roast or grill," said Dermot Murnaghan, and we were off.

The interview itself was a bit of a blur. After about a minute of sitting on my knee, Peeping became restive and began squawking and wriggling about, so I shoved her back in the cat box and began stroking her in a determined "you're not making a run for it" kind of way.

She revenged herself by stamping firmly on the grain-filled margarine container I'd put in the box, so that its contents sprayed the studio floor. Nobody batted an eyelid. Afterwards, I was aware that most of Dermot Murnaghan's questions, phrased in a good-natured, low-intensity teasing manner, seemed to have a theme: eating chicken. Specifically, would I eat Peeping Chicken or any other member of my flock? (No), and did I eat chicken at all? (Yes).

FLESH-EATING CHICKEN

Natasha Kaplinsky asked if she could feed Peeping. I scooped up some of the birdseed, which was still in the travel box, and tipped it into the presenter's hand. Peeping had clearly taken to show business and now ate enthusiastically. Slightly too enthusiastically.

"Oh, ow!" said Natasha, "That was me."

At the far end of the sofa I could see Charles Wheeler, an apparent look of passive incredulity on his face as we plowed on.

The encounter lasted three minutes, and a sense of unreality pervaded the whole thing. An interview like this is something that is done to you—not in an unpleasant way, but you're part of a process, extruded like the product of a sausage factory into people's homes. Then you step off an invisible conveyor belt and emerge back into the real world, blinking with surprise, exactly as you were before.

So, our time was up. Nothing hideous had taken place and cheerful farewells were said. I picked up my chicken and made for the exit. Having scooped up the rest of my clutter, I went and sat in that 1950s foyer.

Peeping continued pecking at the floor of her travel box, intent on eating all the spilled grain that hadn't cascaded out of it. As I sat, people drifted by, their faces registering surprise, amusement, or alarm when they noticed my companion. Staring into the middle distance, I waited for my father to arrive, looked up, and saw Charles Wheeler sail past.

"I like your chicken. I think she's very pretty," he said, the features of his serious face breaking into a huge smile before he vanished down a corridor.

When my father appeared, I swapped a chicken in a box for a black suit on a coat hanger, darted into the nearest loo, changed, and prepared for the day's other big event: a date at Lewisham Crematorium.

2

Three Funerals and a Chicken

A HEN AND KEN

I didn't take a chicken to a funeral by choice. There simply wasn't time to drop her off at home first. I'm not sure Ken Dunbar, the person we were sending off, would have been amused. Perhaps. He had a finely tuned sense of the absurd and might have found it highly entertaining. Then again, he might have been highly pissed off. Ken also had a great capacity for rage, and wasn't slow to express his displeasure. Either way, I could imagine him shaking his head and muttering, "You prick."

I'd known Ken since I was a toddler, and ours was a friendship cemented in the sometimes innocently dysfunctional male world of old cars and old boats. My dad, Ken, and I were a sort of trinity linked by strong cups of tea, the scents of timber, paint, oily things in pieces, river mud, and river water.

Ken was a chunky, apparently permanently middle-aged man, and for me he became part of that retinue of "proper" grown-ups we seem to acquire as we go through life—people we perhaps regard as permanent fixtures in a changing world until time ploughs them into the past, maybe leaving us to assume their "grown-up" roles for others. He possessed a well-cultivated beer belly, Shrek-like features, great comic timing, a collection of original phrases and noises, and a very sharp mind. A big man with a big presence, it seemed odd that he was dead.

Yet it was true. So my dad and I and a chicken made our way to Lewisham Crematorium through central London in my shabby, dull-red Vauxhall Astra, which wafted a slight smell of burning oil into the cabin whenever we were stuck in traffic. It was only mid-morning but the day already seemed to have gone on forever. We'd trundled past Buckingham Palace and were heading to Westminster Bridge. At one of the points where our stop/start progress seemed only to involve stopping, I turned and saw Peeping Chicken take a gurgling drink from the crescent-shaped water container clipped to

the door of her travel box. We eyed each other for a moment, and I thought of the incongruity of her being where she was, where we'd been, and where we were going next.

We arrived an hour and a half early, and then drove up and down the gray-bricked ranks of terraced houses (1930s bay-fronted "Tudor-bethan" creations with ye olde wooden beams, and run-down, boxy 1960s houses), disconsolately looking for a café.

PEEPING'S ARRIVAL

Jane and I had bought Peeping about three months earlier, the morning my father-in-law, Henry, died. It was September and one of those rather beautiful days when the light is pale but the sun hasn't completely lost its strength.

Henry had been ill for a long time, and we had become enmeshed in the dragging inertia of long car journeys to hospitals, of clattering through watery blue or pink corridors smelling of dirt and disinfectant, cheerful bedside conversations and silent bedside vigils.

My wife and I are both children of older parents and some of our friends are much older than we are too, so there's been a sad, natural rate of attrition. When my father-in-law was finally unburdened from a life that had nothing much to do with living, we were triangulating between him and two other deathbeds.

There was Mollie, an ex-neighbor of ours. She was a chain-smoking, seventy-nine-year-old force of nature, with her strong chin and still-dark brown hair pulled back into a tight bun. Ken, too, was a near-seventy-nine-year-old force of nature with a strong chin, but very little hair. Each of these people had become part of the fabric of our lives, and, as illness unraveled that fabric, a lot of my time seemed to involve bizarre shifts from strange episodes promoting a book on hens, to immersion in the grinding, everyday process of dealing with loss. While the former was banal, it did at least offer light relief.

19

That strange juxtaposition arrived with a cell-phone call as we drove to Faversham. The caller was a journalist called Justine Hankins, who wrote a regular pets-related column for *The Guardian* newspaper. It was ten days before *Hen and the Art of Chicken Maintenance* would be launched, and the publishers had arranged the interview, which events had rather driven from our minds.

Explaining that we were actually en route to buy a chicken, we fixed up a time to speak in the afternoon.

At a country fair in Faversham we wandered among the stalls of bric-a-brac and arts-and-crafts items that often seemed entirely artless and completely devoid of craftsmanship, tents filled with ornaments, wooden furniture, and the sort of brassware you can find over a million pub fireplaces, toward the livestock area.

In one marquee we found cages filled with hens of varying sizes and levels of exoticness. This was something of an avian beauty pag-

eant. Prizes were being handed out, but there were also animals for sale, and a sturdy bird who slightly resembled a female grouse stood out.

This was Peeping Chicken, although at the time she was called Jemima. She wasn't fully grown, but had a self-contained calmness, which we liked. Her owner, a man called Dudley Mallett, seemed to have similar qualities, and was very concerned that she went to a good home.

"You won't put her straight in with the rooster, will you?" We assured him that we wouldn't and, after more questions about where she would be housed and how she would be cared for, a deal was done and a cardboard box procured in which a suddenly voluble and reluctant bird was stuffed.

On arriving home, we put Peeping in a pen where our existing birds could see her but couldn't get at her, and found that she was happy to be handfed, which was rather charming.

The phone rang and I did my *Guardian* interview, babbling on about edibility, avian diseases, and the characters of the individual chickens who shared our garden—and whether they had characters at all, a theme that was to recur—all the while conscious that something important had happened to Jane and me, but that it was somehow irrelevant to this mildly ego-stoking moment.

In retrospect I'm not sure that Justine Hankins was convinced that chickens were fun or interesting to have around. At one point she said, "I'm more of a dog person, really," and my attempts to describe the personality quirks of our birds probably came over like the outpourings of a stoned bus enthusiast talking up the fun characteristics of the Leyland Titan double-decker in relation to the Daimler Fleetline. But she was sweet, and her words, when they appeared, were amused, broadly sympathetic, and did not display the perplexity our telephone encounter seemed to imply.

It also seemed to imply that there might be a little respite from the effects of recent events, which as it turned out was anything but the case. Less than a week after that strange, off-kilter Saturday, another hospital was phoning with bad news.

A BOAT AFLOAT

When I was about four, the parents of my contemporaries were driving about in Vauxhall Victors and Triumph Herald cars, but my dad was either in or under a car called a Jowett Javelin. Dating from the 1950s, it proved that terrible alliterative names are nothing new to the motor industry. This car was both ingeniously engineered and chronically unreliable, having a nasty habit of trying to select two gears at once. My father once took another gearbox on holiday, fitting it when we arrived.

There was a sports model called the Jowett Jupiter. Ken Dunbar had one of those, and, appropriately enough, the very first time I saw him it was by the side of the road with the hood up. We were passing in the Javelin on one of the days when it was working properly. We stopped so that my dad could enthusiastically greet a fellow automotive masochist.

The Jowetts didn't endure, but the friendship did, although it became more hit and miss after Ken moved out of his flat and onto a houseboat he'd converted and moored up a high-walled creek just off the river Thames, still in the Brentford/Isleworth hinterland.

When we visited this cozy hideaway, my father and I began to see the appeal of living afloat. Ken eventually found another mooring to rent, which had its own small garden, and his boat could be accessed from the bank without boots when the tide was down, or a dinghy when it wasn't. There was a mooring next to it, and that's where my dad put the boat he'd bought in 1978.

It needed a lot of work, and the words "we'll be on board by Christmas" became a standing joke. It wasn't finished in 1998, when

my dad and I finally moved away. In the meantime, Ken sold his boat and moved into a council flat on the twenty-first floor of a tower block that overlooked the freeway, which sounds grim but wasn't, since the flat was nice, the view fabulous, and the neighbors an interestingly varied bunch.

CAFÉ CULTURE

All these events felt a long way off as my father and I sat in the Lewisham café; we left Peeping in the car, suspecting that the owners wouldn't welcome her presence.

Back in the 1970s Ken was an attendee of an endless series of rough-and-ready cafés in Isleworth and Brentford that would have made this one seem a bit camp. He was a particular fan of a long departed "greasy spoon" café on the main drag in Richmond. A narrow, incredibly dingy space where the walls and windows were sticky with nicotine-brown fat deposits, it looked awful, but the food was great. Hot sweet tea, thick slices of salty bacon, just-cooked mushrooms, and enormous tomatoes. There was nothing insipid about what it offered. Today, I'm sure any self-respecting environmental health officer would have approached the place with a Geiger counter before shutting it down and blowing it up. I loved it, but avoided touching the walls.

Spending time with Ken in these places often meant meeting interesting characters with names such as "Wobbler." Although honest to a fault himself, Ken was happy to pass some of his leisure hours in cafés and pubs alongside people who weren't, or hadn't been in their younger days. One was a simian-faced fifty-something who'd retired from a life of robbery and had a fund of stories that mostly involved getting caught. On one occasion he and some fellow thieves spent hours loading heavy contraband factory equipment into the back of a truck. The cheerful cops who arrested them waited until they'd heaved the very last item onto the truck before making an appearance, then

insisted that the gang offload the whole lot before they carted them down to the lockup.

On another luckier outing they were interrupted on a similar job by a dim-witted officer.

"What are you doing?" boomed the cop.

"Dumping," said one of the gang. This was an inspired piece of lateral thinking.

Showing a skill and judgment that can only be described as re-markable, the policeman replied, "You can't do that. Here, I'll help you load that back on your truck, then you can clear off." He was as good as his word.

Ken had other curious cohorts. There was the world's most bor-ing car mechanic with a foghorn voice, whom he nicknamed "Dink," for reasons I've long since forgotten; and "Smelly Derek," a boat-dwelling thirty-something who'd once worked in higher education or computers—there was certainly something of the dissolute aca-demic about him. Smelly Derek lived on a pretty Dutch barge, hid behind a huge beard, drove a filthy white Lancia sedan, and had such a lack of interest in personal hygiene that it led to a pub ban. Mean-while, another floating near neighbor of Ken's, known as "Big Barry," could be found on an immaculate narrow boat with a dog called Ratbag and a cat called Mucus. Ken was responsible for introducing Barry to the woman he'd eventually marry—naturally, they met in a pub—after which the happy couple set sail up the canal network, never to be seen again.

BEYOND OUR KEN

Ken was a serial monogamist with the local pubs, walking the foot-paths to bestow his custom on a particular boozer for a while, before moving off to one of its rivals. Go to a pub with Ken and you tended

to be one of the last to leave, and the journey home along the foot-path, which might normally have taken fifteen minutes, could be drawn out for a couple of hours.

There would be stops to piddle, benches on which to sit, things to talk about, cashless little wagers on when a defective streetlight on the other bank of the river would flash next. He'd been married, but it had ended unhappily for reasons that were never discussed, as there was always a part of Ken's personality that kept its distance.

He was a sociable man who sometimes liked to pull up the draw-bridge and shut out the wider world when it suited him. When that happened you backed off and left him to it, or ran the risk of being on the receiving end of a volcanic, expletive-laden eruption of temper.

If you spent time in Ken's company you did so on his terms, and there might be long gaps when you didn't see him at all.

So, when Dad and I met him again in a pub on Kew Green, the three-year space since we'd seen him last wasn't commented on. Ken was thinner, with big hands and feet that seemed out of proportion to the rest of him, but the flow of conversation was the same as ever.

I'd brought along a copy of the chicken book. Ken usually took the wind out of my writing efforts as an automotive journalist. The very first thing I'd had published had been a one-page article on an old Fiat, culled entirely from research, since I hadn't actually seen the car or driven it.

"How many wheel nuts has it got, then?" chortled Ken. He could spot an armchair expert at a thousand paces, but when it came to the chicken book he was benign, and I promised to send him a copy. Having his approval was a surprise, and oddly important.

The three of us shared pleasantly familiar reminiscences, such as the festive occasion of my dad arriving on Ken's boat one Christmas clasping a bottle of Scotch, greeting him warmly before slipping and

putting his foot through a galley window. Later, Ken mentioned that he'd joined the cricket club on Kew Green, as a spectator rather than a participant.

"They baked a cake for my last birthday, and I got a birthday kiss from all the wives. Lovely," he said with undisguised glee.

"How do you think he looked?" my dad asked afterwards.

"Not bad," I lied.

"I thought so too," he lied back.

I phoned Ken the following week. It was the usual exchange of verbal daftness, during which I mentioned some minor ailment I'd suffered.

"I've not been so well, actually," said Ken. "Went to the hospital last week. I've felt a bit strange and breathless."

He'd sat on a gurney at the West Middlesex Hospital, admiring the nurses, was given a variety of tests and chest X-rays, then told he could go home.

I had to visit London the following week and said that I'd call on him.

"I just can't do anything. It's so bloody frustrating," said Ken.

SEEN AND HURD

The purpose of my London visit was to talk about the book. The publishers had lined up some radio interviews, and Catherine, one of their publicity people, would be chaperoning me at Broadcasting House. At the time, the idea of doing these things with a hen hadn't suggested itself, so I arrived solo. Once admitted into the bowels of the building we drank vile coffee, then joined a sort of mini conga line of book pluggers, including Douglas Hurd, the grandee Tory politician, whose hair, while clearly attached to his head in all the right places, twizzled upwards in a fascinating way, and a bald man whom I later realized was Oz Clark, the wine-drinking television guy.

To commune with BBC Radio Jersey, among others, I was dispatched to a series of rooms the size of toilet cubicles, each containing a chair and a desk, on which was a sort of sound mixing desk arrangement, a microphone, a pair of headphones, and a green lamp that looked like a giant egg. A clock was attached to one of the walls.

Feeling slightly sweaty, I'd put on the headphones to find myself plugged into the sound of chatter, jingles, and the sort of pop music that, like old soldiers, never dies, but draws its pension playing on provincial radio stations. Immerse yourself in the world of local music radio and you will be pitched back ten-, twenty-, thirty-plus years, courtesy of artists you sometimes might have tried hard to forget.

Local radio will remind you that period poodle soft rocker Michael Bolton always sang like a male steer that had woken up midway through a nasty medical procedure, and that early Mariah Carey songs had all the emotional rawness of shrink-wrapped plastic. You may have forgotten their aural bleatings, but be warned: smooth-talkin' DJ Barry Dross, denizen of the seminal "Good Morning San Bernardino" show, will be more than happy to transport you back to mid-1990s musical hell. Frankly, as you read these words, someone, somewhere is playing "In the Jungle"; not the original, but the version put out by one-hit wonders Tight Fit, an early-1980s boy/girl band who couldn't dance and wore stylish leopard-skin diapers. Are Tight Fit still active on the touring circuit? Are they still called Tight Fit, or has time meant rechristening themselves as "Loose Tremor"? Life is cruel, and today those diapers would probably be useful.

CH-CH-CH-CHICKENS

Old David Bowie songs have become local radio staples too, and, as I spoke to more of these stations, one—"Changes"—seemed to follow me around.

It turned up several times as I waited to engage in hilarious banter with radio anchor people about why we don't eat our pet chickens, and it made an appearance immediately before one of these interviews.

"That was 'Ch-ch-ch-changes,' by David Bowie," said the deejay in one of those smooth, mannered "Hi, girls" voices that put the listener in mind of beige golfing slacks. Then he added, "And now, ch-ch-ch-Chickens!"

It was hard to know quite what to say after that.

Some of the other questions I've been asked during these encounters have also been a bit difficult to parry. A frequent variation on the "Do you eat your chickens?" one has been "Do you eat your chickens after they are dead?"

What do you think? Eating them beforehand isn't much of an option. They wriggle when they're alive, the feathers are likely to get stuck between your teeth, and the process itself might be a little distressing for both parties, so we wouldn't eat them at that point. Once they've shuffled off their mortal perches the presence of death tends to indicate that they weren't well beforehand.

"Sickly corpse for supper, dear?"

"Mmmm, sounds lovely!"

The nature of this question tends to imply that the questioner hasn't entirely thought it through. Normally, it doesn't pay to think too deeply about these things yourself, so when asked I would just say no and wait for the next inquiry.

MAVIS'S TAXING QUESTIONS

One interview that completely threw me took place after a long, inconclusive phone-in about the evils of local taxation. Is there a mad scientist somewhere minting genetically modified nitwits who want to phone these things and talk balls, or are we the subject of an alien invasion from the far-off galaxy of Moronosphere, a place populated by aliens who want to enslave us in a netherworld of perpetual banality?

"Soon, Earthling scum, your puny thought waves will be under our control. You will all believe that you want to eat at Harvester restaurants and vote for the UK Independence Party."

Sorry. I seem to have wandered from the point somewhat. We were talking about council-tax-related radio phone-ins. The one taking place before my book-flogging interview went something like this:

"Now we have Mavis Lobotomy. What's your point, Mavis?"

Long pause.

"Mavis?"

"Hello? Hello? Oh, yes. Local tax."

"Yes, Mavis, what's your point?"

"I pay it."

"And?"

"Well, I don't like to, do I?"

When they got around to me, the DJ slickly segued to his chicken-related theme by asking,

"So, Martin, what do you think of local tax?"

"Er."

Later, Catherine from Publicity said it had gone OK. At least talking to local radio presenters was less of a challenge than the one facing her boyfriend, who at the time was earning a living in advertising. He was trying to write song lyrics about a free handbag to go with every Barbie doll sold by a big toy store—with many of the words (such as "Barbie" and "bag," one presumes) pre-supplied. How embarrassing is *that*?

With this thought in mind, I headed for Ken's flat in Brentford. He claimed to be feeling a little better, but as I sat glumly at Kew Bridge station a couple of hours later, I knew he wasn't.

A press trip was bringing me back to London the following week and we arranged that I would see him then. Meanwhile, my wife and I were planning to travel to Essex for the weekly visit to our friend Mollie.

SILK CUTS AND CARROTS

Mollie lived in a small Victorian house in Braintree, where her parents and grandparents had lived before her.

When we moved in next door, Mollie was a feisty, chain-smoking sixty-nine-year-old with a neat strip of garden that gave way to a vegetable patch of extreme tidiness and produced huge heads of lettuce and sweet, corkscrew-shaped carrots.

Her world revolved around the rhythms of shopping, market days, old films, snooker, or Wimbledon on the television, when the coalman or the window cleaner was visiting, family birthdays, and the annual painting-and-decorating spree that saw another coat of pale-green paint applied to the walls of her small sitting room.

A rainstorm, a shared leaking roof, and a night spent with buckets, mops, cups of coffee, and eventually—because we were all too wired up to sleep—several hours spent looking at holiday photos with a lot of inconsequential chatter really brought Jane, Mollie, and me together. We just got on.

When we moved away, the friendship actually strengthened. Socializing with neighbors often has a lot to do with proximity. No longer living next door, we would come back several times a year, and these visits became special. They also took on a ritualistic pattern.

We would arrive later than planned and present Mollie with half a dozen eggs. She would ask after the birds and say how good her previous eggs had been. (Mollie believed in the health-giving properties of a raw egg mixed into a glass of milk for breakfast.)

Then we would drive to a pub and argue over who was paying the bill. Back at the house, gin and cigs would be produced, with which Mollie and Jane would make increasingly merry, and our dog would be indulged with sausages. Despite the pub lunch, by teatime Mollie would insist on feeding us again, either with butter-laden white bread and tongue sandwiches (from which the crusts had been cut and bagged up for our chickens), or strange pizzas with thick bases and toppings that often seemed to involve cheddar cheese and pineapple pieces. Mollie wouldn't touch them, thinking they were weird, exotic foodstuffs that only "young people" liked eating. "Yeaugh! No, thank you," she would cry before shoving enormous slices at us.

You did not say "no" to Mollie. "I wouldn't offer if I didn't want you to have it, so you can shut up about it now," she'd say before stomping into the kitchen on a booze- or food-replenishing mission.

Gradually, we would be pulled into the comic, sad, or passively malicious gossip that partially fuels life in a provincial street, in this case involving the doings and alleged misdeeds of people who seemed to acquire nicknames, including "The Rear Admiral" and a lady referred to as "I was just looking out of the window" (as in "'I was just looking out of the window' told me that she'd seen . . ."). We heard about decamping wives, defective cats, despicable daughters, or the latest racing triumphs or disasters of a horse called Uncle Ernie.

Gentle hints at 7 P.M. that we would have to make a move "soon" usually meant a reluctant departure two hours later, laden with bags containing empty egg cartons that Mollie had been saving for us.

Jane and the dog, blitzed (respectively) on gin and sausages, would spend most of the journey home happily unconscious.

Old age never made Mollie infirm. It just slowed her down and got in her way. Our visits were still cheerful, boozy occasions, but eventually the smoking caught up with her. There had been a persistent cough, three months of nonspecific illness, and a refusal to let us visit, then a phone call from a neighbor. Mollie was in the hospital.

"I've got lung cancer," she said when we clattered onto the open ward. "I guess it's sink or swim."

She swam, putting up with a battery of tests, joking with nurses and consultants ("Oh, you've come to puncture me again, have you? Any more of this and I'll spring a leak"), shamelessly eavesdropping on the conversations of other patients and their relatives, and making none-too-subtle comments about their vices and virtues.

TATTIE TÊTE-À-TÊTE

Each week Jane and I clomped through the 1950s-to-1980s mess of a hospital complex to her bedside, where we were able to dispense gin and lemonade and freezer-bagged garden tomatoes, which she regarded as antidotes to the warmed-over industrial sludge that passed as food.

Once we listened in awed silence to a pair of huge, wheezing diabetic women in opposing beds.

"I like Yorkshires. Yes there's nothing like a nice Yorkshire."

"Yorkshires? Yes I like a nice Yorkshire."

"And tatties."

"Tatties? Tatties? Yes I *love* tatties. Nothing like a nice tattie. How do you like your tatties? I like mine roasted."

"Roasted tatties. That's what I like. Roasties."

"Roasties. Yeah, roasties. What's for supper, then?"

"Dunno. Hope it's sausages. I like sausages, I do. A good sausage. You can't beat a good sausage."

"I like my meat."

"You know what I like?"

"No, what?"

"Rump. I like a nice bit of rump, that's what I like. There's nothing like a nice bit of rump."

Soon, liking "a nice bit of rump" became another in-joke, and, three months and a couple of hospital moves later, Mollie went home. Everyone knew that the disease had spread, but she rallied, gained weight, and looked both well and happy. She was definitely swimming rather than sinking.

We saw Mollie every weekend, and our feelings about those visits changed from trepidation to anticipation. Her health seemed to be on a gentle, constant upward curve. During this time Ken and Henry had fared less well. Once, when we were visiting Mollie, my cell

phone rang. It was a nurse from the small, old-fashioned cottage hospital in Teddington where my father-in-law was being looked after. "I think you should come today."

So we made our excuses, and—instead of driving back to rural Kent, our garden and animals and a bottle of wine—headed along the highway to the North Circular Road, past the flats near Henley's Corner (which all seem to have chandeliers), made our way through the semipermanent traffic jam between Hanger Lane and Chiswick, and out to Teddington to the heavy, suspended animation of the small side room where Henry had been moved.

Fourteen days later, when we made a similar journey, very little had apparently changed, except that everything else we had to get on with seemed more of an effort, whether it was writing, shopping, or cleaning out the henhouse.

THE BELLS, THE BELLS!

I had talked to several more local radio stations about why it was that we didn't eat our chickens, and to say yes, they did have individual personalities, and no, I did not know why the chicken crossed the road, and what a fabulous joke that was. "Ha" and, indeed, "Ha!"

During this time a telephone interview was arranged with Danny Baker's *London Live* early morning radio show. To prepare for this I spent the previous evening getting plastered, and woke with a raging headache and a lightly fluttering eyelid, thanks to a trapped nerve.

When they phoned I was still in bed, and can now remember almost nothing about what took place, except that at the end they asked me to name the chickens we owned then, and each time one was mentioned they rang a bell.

"Tikka!"

Ding!

"Baggy Chicken!"

Ding!

"Er, Elvis!"

Ding!

"Bossy Chicken!"

Ding!

"Mrs. Brown!"

Ding!

(Hungover author screws up face and concentrates.)

"Delia!"

Ding!

"Satan!"

Ding!

And so on. For some reason I had great difficulty remembering their names, and realized afterwards that at least two of the birds I'd named had keeled over a long time beforehand.

RIBENA AND MILDEW

I'd taken to phoning Ken on a daily basis. My father-in-law died two days before a press trip I was using as an excuse to visit him again.

A classic car magazine had asked me to spend a couple of days in the company of some Rolls-Royce and Bentley owners on a wine-tasting trip in France, and I'd arranged to see Ken en route to Heathrow. He'd asked me to buy basic provisions from the local supermarket, and some rolling tobacco. I didn't argue about this.

At his flat I made some tea as Ken sprawled in a battered armchair. He looked exhausted, and I had the uncomfortable feeling that, for the first time, I had assumed the role of adult. I headed for the airport and forty-eight hours in the company of some jolly old car owners having a nice time in an expensive French château. The comment of one about a dignified bottle of ancient red—"Ugh! It tastes like fruit punch and mildew"—will live with me for a long time.

When I next tried calling Ken, the phone kept ringing. Back home, Jane offered to contact the local hospital; she soon discovered that this was where he was, and she even got to speak to him—I felt relieved.

Back home, I talked to a journalist from *The Independent*, who was writing a story about chicken-keeping. "Do hens have personalities? Would you eat any of your flock?" she asked. Later a nurse from the hospital rang. Ken had fallen and struck his head on a sink. It wasn't good; they couldn't find any family members; could I help? Oh, yes, and would I act as next of kin?

As events telescoped, it was hard to write or think about amusing chicken-related anecdotes connected with the book, which was by then days away from going on sale. I took a shovel and cleaned out the chicken run. It was something to do that involved physical exercise and not much thought. As the birds scuttled around my boots clucking excitedly and yanking unfortunate worms out of the turned-over ground, I dug and howled.

That evening Jane and I made an eighty-mile dash to the West Middlesex Hospital. Ken was moribund and unable to speak. Afterwards, in a clinically comfortable hospital waiting room, an impossibly young-looking doctor told us what we knew already, and asked if I wanted a cup of tea. I told him I wanted to escape from the hospital as quickly as I could and perhaps find a pub.

"I can understand that," he said.

They phoned the following morning to tell us Ken had died.

PIECES OF EIGHT, PIECES OF EIGHT!

In the middle of all this I discovered that Peeping Chicken was happy to stand on my shoulder like a very fat parrot. We teamed up in the back garden having our pictures taken for the *Independent* piece, with Peeping peering into the middle distance or entertaining herself by

yanking at my hair with her beak, much to the photographer's amusement, and, despite feeling as if my nerve endings had been flayed with a wire brush, I'd started wondering about taking this docile animal out and about as a means of promoting the book.

Would it be cruel? Not necessarily, if the travel box she traveled in was spacious, there was plenty of food, water, and treats, and the journeys were punctuated with breaks.

Once, on a long weekend in Norfolk, I'd seriously considered taking along a chicken whose legs had gone on strike, so that she could be medicated and exercised. However, Jane had visions of the bird stinking her car out and having to explain to the owners of a pathologically neat bed and breakfast why we were traveling with a chicken. Nevertheless, with a healthy hen and a reason for her to be in my company far from home, this didn't seem such a problem.

Where could we go? More or less anywhere, but bookshops seemed a good starting point. It was a cheap stunt, but that was part of the appeal, and when Southern Counties Radio got in touch I asked if they wanted a feathered interviewee to go with the human one. They seemed to think this was a good idea.

At some stage in all this mélange, the book went on sale, we buried my father-in-law, and one of my dad's shoes "exploded" at the funeral. As we stood outside Mortlake Crematorium he noticed a certain draftiness around his left foot, looked down, and saw that both the stitching and leather of the shoe had torn away, and lay flapping, jagged and exhausted, around a now exposed green sock. It looked as if a tiny bomb had blown the shoe apart.

My dad, stepmother, Jane, and I were in a sort of chilly huddle. We looked down and were quietly seized by the mild hysteria created by a funny event taking place in an otherwise deeply serious setting. It was, it seemed, all right to acknowledge this.

DOUBLE TROUBLE

For our radio debut as a duo, Peeping Chicken and I traveled to Guildford—she in the old cat box that had once been used by the other chickens when my home office was a former garden wash house and the birds found themselves short of an egg-laying place; both of us in the $125 Vauxhall Astra that was my regular everyday car. Both conveyances were weary, frayed at the edges, and a bit naff, but they did the job.

Peeping turned out to be a calm passenger, sitting on some straw in the cat box and apparently finding the process of my changing gear mildly interesting, as she studied my left hand intently through the grille in the side of her travel box. When this ceased to hold her attention she would peck at the food in the bottom of her mobile home, or drink from its water container; I took these things to be a sign that she wasn't particularly stressed.

We arrived early. I spread some newspaper on my lap, fished some raisins from a packet wedged among the old pens, screws, Post-it notes, and general "stuff" that ends up in my car's center console, extracted a complaining chicken, planted her on my knee, and offered her a handful of dried fruit. After about three seconds' deliberation she began eating.

I'd parked in a side street, which was surprisingly busy, with a constant flow of pedestrians promenading past our car. Old Vauxhall Astras are the last word in vehicular anonymity, and nobody seemed to notice the odd goings-on in this one, which was just as well. A credible explanation would have been difficult.

"Why have you got a chicken in your car?"

"We're going to do a radio interview."

"Of course you are."

Well, we did the interview and nothing disastrous happened. Peeping Chicken sat on my lap, ate raisins, and didn't crap on my trousers. Were we asked about whether I'd eat one of my flock, or whether they had different personalities? I honestly can't remember. A general feeling of affability is my abiding recollection.

Afterwards, somebody from the studio appeared with a digital camera. Could they have a picture of the DJ and Peeping Chicken?

Having handed over my slightly nonplussed fellow traveler, I waited as she was planted on a sound board. Peeping wasn't fazed by the camera flash, retained her admirable bowel control in the proximity of electrical equipment, and didn't adjust any of the fader switches with her claws. (By the way, is it true that in the 1920s BBC radio engineers reversed these controls so that if some unfortunate, dinner-jacketed announcer croaked mid-sentence and fell forward onto his mixing board, he'd fade himself out in every sense?)

Since the studio was in Guildford, after Peeping and I had said our good-byes, we set off for the village of Shamley Green and my chain-smoking Great-Aunt Nora, then a very determined 102 years old. Age had given her a frail, shell-like quality and largely robbed her of mobility (she'd had a hip replacement at eighty-nine and was still gardening on her hands and knees at ninety-eight), but a mix of resolute atheism, a sharp mind, and, well, determination had kept her going. She was a contemporary person who happened to have been around for a long time, and despite her great age, this was a person who was very much alive, which made her something of a human tonic.

Having left Peeping in the car, I gave Nora half a dozen eggs. She lit up, thanked me, and said she'd read the book.

"You didn't disapprove?" I asked. (It contained a fair smattering of latrine-level humor and a fat selection of swear words. I wondered what this patrician, centenarian *Daily Telegraph* reader had made of "fuckshit.")

"Disapprove of what?" she asked, fixing me with one of her beadier looks.

"The language."

"Oh, *that*," she said, dismissively waggling a tiny hand. "That's just you. I'm just pleased you've written something. You always talked about it, but I didn't think you ever would."

I asked if she'd like to meet Peeping Chicken. The idea seemed to amuse her. The cat box was extracted from the car and Peeping was brought before the Presence. I was conscious of a certain farmyard odor, but didn't belabor the point.

"Does it lay eggs?" asked Nora.

"Not yet," I said.

"Well, that's not much good, then. She'll be for the pot."

My great-aunt didn't attempt to pet her feathered guest, but made complimentary noises about her plumage. We talked about the idea of my going out on the road to promote the book with Peeping, which caused Nora to laugh a lot.

"Well," she said doubtfully, "why not?"

When I left this diminutive, elegant person, wreathed as usual in cigarette smoke, I too thought, *Why not?* The idea quickly grew and fermented, plans were pulled together and arrangements made— which is why I found myself at Lewisham Crematorium on a damp November afternoon, with my dad and Peeping Chicken, preparing to say good-bye to Ken Dunbar, having started the day sharing a sofa with Peeping and Natasha Kaplinsky.

PEEPING AT PEEPING

As Peeping remained in her car-bound cat box, pecking at the lumpy bits of white bread my father and I had saved for her from our café meal, a small huddle of Ken's friends and family were going through the motions of a low-key, low-fuss funeral that was practically a disposal process.

The coffin sat on a sort of giant marble work surface, into which, at the appropriate moment, it began to sink, accompanied by a low, mechanical rumble. It looked like a figurine on a giant musical box. This stagy, Cecil B. DeMille exit seemed about as far removed from

Ken's personality as it was possible to imagine. Only putting a top hat and cane on the coffin lid could have added to the moment.

Afterwards some of the mourners asked to meet Peeping Chicken, as we trudged through the crematorium parking lot. Everyone huddled around the Astra and made cooing noises before we headed for the nearest pub, a large, shabby edifice populated by raddled-looking men with alcoholic complexions and staffed by people who seemed hardly more cheerful than we were. I asked a hatchet-faced barmaid about bringing animals into the pub.

"What sort of animal is it?" she scowled.

"A chicken. In a basket."

She was a study of floral-aproned disdain. "We don't allow dogs in here, so we certainly wouldn't allow chickens."

I asked for a half of Guinness.

"Two down, one to go," I found myself saying to my dad later as we drove home. Mollie had died the week before. She'd kept swimming almost until the very end.

So, when we made our way to Essex for funeral number three, we felt a mixture of sadness and release. There would at last be time for other things and, at least for a while, life wouldn't solely be shaped and driven by crap events. So, the next time somebody asked me if our chickens had individual personalities and whether we would be prepared to feast on them, I'd respond with a sunnier disposition. Frankly, had I been the journalist asking the questions rather than answering them, these two would have been near the top of my list.

It was likely that I was going to carry on being asked. *Hen* had done well enough to make organizing some book signings worthwhile, and a number of low-key "bird and author" gigs had been penciled in. However socially inadequate this may sound, I'd found

the book's apparent success and the attention it brought flattering, exciting, and in its way, sustaining. Who wouldn't?

It felt as if I'd come to the end of an exhausting, difficult journey. The trip I was about to make would be neither of those things, just rather peculiar, and the company would be better. I was keen to get started.

3

A Chapter
About Chickens

COUNTING OUR CHICKENS

This is a book about chickens, which so far has featured one bird in a slightly oblique way. It's time to put this right.

We keep seven hens. There's Egghead, a venerable, sit-down chicken with ruffles under her chin, who has gradually been transformed from screeching twerp to imperious dowager. Then there's Tikka, an ex-farm bird who conceals her relatively advanced age (she's at least four) with a refusal to retire from laying eggs and some rather pretty plumage. They live with Peeping Chicken, the well-traveled Buff Sussex, who has grown stocky and matronly. Then there's Aloe and Vera, a pair of beady hens. They're both Neras (a breed), who take great pleasure in bullying Beryl, a battered-looking, standard working chicken with a clipped beak and a mysterious past. Finally, there's Sven the rooster, a handsome, allegedly Swedish bird who is, frankly, a bit of a wuss.

If you've read this book's predecessor, then only the first two names will be familiar, and you might want a bit of a progress report. If not, bear with me anyway. I'm writing these words nearly three years after finishing *Hen*, and there have inevitably been some departures, so let's get these out of the way.

Our flock, as it was, consisted of Mrs. Brown, Elvis, Egghead, Tikka, Delia, Baggy, and Hendon—the last four were also known as "the stringy quartet," and were bought secondhand from a free-range chicken farm. This meant we had no idea how old the foursome were, and in the course of a year the Grim Reaper worked his way through their ranks until Tikka went solo.

MRS. BROWN'S NAMESAKE

Mrs. Brown was one of our favorite birds, a determined "in charge" animal who used to break into the house and pinch the cat's dinner, would sometimes sit on laps, and liked following us around the garden.

She laid the most enormous, fist-sized eggs, until one broke inside her and she nearly died. The vet gave her a vicious shot of antibiotics and handed me a swathe of further medication, and said that we'd be lucky if Mrs. B lasted for twenty-four hours. She kept going for another happy three and a bit years, laying infrequently, then not at all, suffering occasional relapses, which meant further medication, and racking up an impressive stack of vet bills. She cost $6.50 to buy and about $137 to keep going, but her strength of personality made this seem a good value for the money.

Are you thinking, "Why did these idiot people spend a hundred and forty dollars on a chicken?" There are two answers. One is simply that we could, so we did; the other is that we bought her as a pet rather than as livestock. Would you bump off the family budgie if the bird became ill and it was going to cost a bit to get it put right at the vet's?

Mrs. Brown had a ball: bossing the other hens around, eating copiously (she was a practiced murderer of garden snails and slugs), and giving her human slaves a particular sideways "What have you got for me, then?" look, which usually resulted in our proffering something edible.

She keeled over one Valentine's night, having spent the day eating and scratching about as normal. By then she was a rather grand old lady, and although we were sorry that she was no longer around, we felt a certain satisfaction at her longevity. We were also rather charmed to discover that Mrs. Brown has a namesake. I was writing a story for *The Independent* about urban chicken keepers and placed an ad in a magazine called *Smallholder* asking for interviewees. One of the people who phoned was a lady who'd read about Mrs. Brown's life and times, and decided to name one of her flock after the old worm tugger.

Mrs. B was easily outpaced in the life span stakes by Elvis. I'm writing this just a few weeks after she finally wore out. How old was she then? Seven, eight years old at least. We were never sure, but she was adult and laying when we bought her.

Elvis, the girl chicken with the boy's name, was always rather butch, and to start with a bit confused genderwise, half crowing when life was especially exciting or stressful. This hormonal angst seemed to settle down after a bit, but she continued to regard all human beings as deeply alarming and as sources of scuttling-about terror if they went anywhere near her. She was rather pretty, with shining black feathers, which she shed at regular intervals. In moments of extreme tension (and Elvis was highly strung), clumps of them would drop out, leaving her with great bald patches and a sort of feathery stubble as her new ones emerged, quill-like in their protective tubes.

She went to the vet only twice. The first time was when she'd engaged in one of these instant molts and looked as if she were at

least half oven-ready. We were a lot more naive at the time, and the vet kindly pointed out the bald patches were nothing to worry about. Chickens were meant to do this sort of thing. The next visit was when it was clear that even she had finally run out of time.

THE MARK OF ZORRO

We hadn't expected Zorro the rooster to fall off the twig. A swaggering swathe of golds, greens, and blacks who protected his ladies from human visitors by attacking their boots or jumping up and down on their hands if they tried to remove eggs from the egg nest when he was nearby, he was a vigorous, fit-looking extrovert.

Then, one New Year's Eve morning, I found him looking distinctly off-color in a nonspecific way, hunched and immobile in the corner of the henhouse. A trip to Julia, our ever-patient vet, was arranged. Zorro was uncharacteristically cooperative, and it was discovered that he was running a temperature, so he was given an injection of antibiotics. A few minutes after that he collapsed.

"Shock," said Julia.

He was carted into a treatment room and I ended up cradling his head in one hand and pointing a small oxygen tube at his nostrils with the other. After a while, he revived but remained weak and woozy, so the vet, bless her, offered to take him home with her over New Year's, and I left them to it.

Later that day the phone rang. It was Julia again. "I'm afraid Zorro has passed away," she said. It seemed an incongruous way to put it.

So, we entered the New Year with an unscheduled rooster vacancy, but it's amazing how Fate can spot a vacuum and instantly fill it. A few days later I was slaving over a journalistic magnum opus on something about holiday car rentals when the phone rang.

THE MAN IN THE GINGERBREAD HOUSE

"I haf read about your book about ze chickens," said a man with a foreign accent. "And I think ve should go into business together."

I asked exactly what he had in mind.

"I live in Britain but I come from Sweden, and I vant to import and breed Swedish fancy chickens. I think ve should vork together doing this," said the voice, which belonged to someone who turned out to live in a house on the outskirts of our village.

He'd already started a breeding program, which had been very successful in terms of the number of chicks raised, but had left him with seventeen roosters and a noise-related dispute with his next-door neighbor. I told him that I wasn't up for a career change involving Swedish chicken importation, but if he had a spare rooster, we could give it a home.

Our new friend lived in a sort of gingerbread cottage, around which swarms of quite exotic, unfamiliar-looking birds pottered about. The job of choosing a rooster was made a lot easier by the fact that most of them were lining up on the next-door neighbor's garden fence, backsides dangling over his roses, the better to manure them with acrid, acid guano.

A local firm of commercial chicken breeders had offered to take most of them—for what purpose we preferred not to ask—but we could pick more or less any bird we wanted. We eventually settled on a broad-chested individual with an attractive mixture of white, gold, and dark-red, almost wine-colored, feathers. Later that afternoon a Volvo station wagon pulled up outside our house, and the putative Swedish chicken baron appeared, carrying a cardboard box. We christened its contents "Sven."

Some roosters can be vicious, chasing their owners, pecking and slashing at them with sharp, curling spurs. Zorro would have slightly half-hearted goes at domestic violence against human visitors, but

usually ran away if you stood your ground. In extremis, when his hormones went ballistic, picking him up and cuddling him was the last word in humiliation.

Sven just runs away. He's bigger and, if anything, more butch than Zorro, but seems convinced that you're about to disassemble him like a defective Ikea flat pack. That he always keeps his distance suits us fine.

COCKSURE

Both Sven and Zorro shared that rooster thing of shagging as many of their girlfriends as possible when they're first let out of the henhouse and then looking for breakfast. Male chickens are not considerate lovers. They like short, frequent quickies, and their idea of foreplay involves a running jump. If you're a rooster and there's food about, and the object of your desire is busy eating it and has her back turned to you, so much the better.

Zorro had a habit of pointing out tidbits for his ladies, and quite often seemed to forget about eating, which we thought was charming, until it was pointed out to us by somebody in the know that some roosters did this as a way of getting members of their harem exactly where they wanted them. It wasn't a case of gentlemanly behavior, more one of peck and plook.

In this respect Sven is less of a cad, but his conflict-resolution skills are somewhat lacking.

Chickens operate under strict pecking orders, and the further down the social scale you are the more you will be pecked, and for some birds at the bottom of the heap, life can be pretty nasty. Zorro would ignore swift beak batterings at mealtimes, but generally waded in if there was more sustained bullying. However, Sven just doesn't seem to notice, which has not been good news for Beryl, a runt in chicken form.

With her slightly lopsided beak, which somebody has clipped, and permanently battered plumage, Beryl is not conventionally beautiful. In terms of genealogy, she is a standard, brown "hybrid" farm chicken, but a bit undersized. Add to this a nervous disposition, and you have a genetically engineered victim.

We didn't go looking for this egg-laying bundle of nerves; she found us. The vet had been contacted by a family who had rescued the unfortunate bird, but had nowhere to keep her, and wanted to pass Beryl on to someone who had.

An electrician friend of theirs had been working on a building site trailer, crawled underneath it to fix some wiring, and found himself sharing this confined space with what seemed to be a dead chicken lying in a puddle. Deciding that he didn't want his working environment to contain a corpse, he started to remove it, and the apparently lifeless animal twitched. The family had saved a number of wild birds, so, when their friend arrived with a sick chicken in a sack, a cure was effected using a hairdryer, and she quickly revived, although it took two or three days for her to dry out entirely.

They christened her Beryl, a name that really suits the bird, and moved her into their garden shed, which contained the usual household clutter of bicycles, tools, and paint cans, and, having decided that these things didn't go well with a chicken, they called the vet to ask about finding her a new home, and the vet called us.

BERYL IN PERIL

I met Beryl a few days before Christmas, and, having promised that the skinny beast wouldn't be for the pot, took her home, putting her in a separate run so that our existing birds could get to know her from a safe distance, and as a means of keeping her apart from them should she be carrying any diseases.

Usually new arrivals are given the eye by henhouse old inmates for about a week; then it's safe to start introducing them to the others. Not so Beryl, who was on the receiving end of a lot of cold stares and impotent attempts at pecking through the wire mesh of her separate enclosure. It took about three weeks for things to start settling down and, eventually, just as the birds were roosting, I put her in with our existing hens.

The following morning there were no obvious signs of bullying, but soon afterwards the animus began to be ramped up, accompanied by distressed squawking noises from Beryl, who within a few days was being harassed 90 percent of the time. When Sven arrived, he did nothing to stop it. For a while it was back to the cooler for Beryl, so that the other hens could give her nothing worse than dirty looks.

We gave it another couple of weeks, then reintroduced her, and everyone picked up from where they'd left off, particularly Aloe, the chicken who was third from the bottom in the pecking order and an enthusiastic bully, having adopted that playground approach of doing it to somebody else so that it doesn't get done to you.

Her violent *pièce de résistance* was to have a go at Beryl while she was being bonked by Sven, yanking at the poor bird's neck feathers while she was squashed into the floor of the run. Something had to be done.

Our chicken house is an adapted garden shed with two home-made aviary areas, one at either side. We'd been given an old rabbit hutch and had put it in one of the aviaries, and this is currently occupied by Beryl and Egghead, our most elderly chicken, who these days doesn't do much in the way of walking, making her a sitting target for Sven's lascivious activities.

SHAGGED OUT?

Egghead is technically at the top of the pecking order, the diametric opposite of Beryl, but she really can't work up the energy to give

Beryl a hard time. She just sits like a sagging, feather-clad hot-water-bottle cozy, blinking myopically as her still slightly demented cohabitee hurtles around. To be fair, Beryl is becoming less like a Ping-Pong ball by the day, and has even begun to grow new feathers.

We're not quite sure what to do with these two. Eight months ago, Egghead went through a period when she couldn't be bothered to get off her perch and eat. I used to assist her twice a day. She would totter about, then sit and look at everyone else eating. She gradually weakened and started to give up. One evening I found her still sitting outside when the others had roosted, so I separated her, proffered large quantities of tinned sweet corn, which quickly rekindled her interest in greed, and then embarked on some assisted walking by clasping her wings and gently cycling her backwards and forwards like a carpet sweeper.

This worked up to a point. Egghead now walked short distances to food, ate when she arrived, and then sat down and did nothing. Naturally, Sven viewed Egghead's relative inability to run away as a great plus.

I'd heard Francine Raymond, author of *A Few Hens in the Garden*, giving a radio interview in which she described how one of her favorite chickens died of a heart attack after a particularly vigorous bonking, and I thought something similar had happened to poor old Egghead after a rugby-game-style coupling that left her prone and immobile for a few seconds.

After that, I organized separate accommodations for her and Beryl, where the other birds can still see them, and I suspect this is how things will remain.

Hidden costs

As for Aloe and Vera, they ended up costing me about $150 each. We bought them from a local breeder. We wanted a couple of pretty birds that would lay regularly and often, and last longer than the brown "hybrid" farm hens, which mature rapidly and wear out fast. Given Mrs. Brown's medical needs and the speedy exit of three of the Stringy Quartet, this seemed like a sensible move.

The farm was accessed down a rutted track and had a variety of breeds. We hadn't heard of Neras, but liked the look of these two. They, themselves, had cost less than $20 each, but there was a hidden extra that was going to cost me. With our two prizes sitting in a cardboard box, I began navigating my wife's relatively youthful Subaru station wagon back down the rutted track. One of those tiny, buzzing Japanese panel vans was coming the other way and, since there was room for only one vehicle, I pulled into what looked like a passing place. The old metal gatepost was completely hidden

by foliage, and made itself known only when I crunched the side of the car into it.

"Oh bother," I said (this bit is made up, although what was actually said *did* start with the word "Oh"). My wife was professionally understanding, and I was significantly poorer.

Both Aloe and Vera produce eggs with assembly-line efficiency, even if Aloe soon went partially bald. I thought the rooster was to blame—think "friction"—then mites, but the bird has endured regular squirtings of budgie-tick repellent to no obvious effect. The vet thought Aloe was stuck in mid-molt, and I spent a happy week rubbing medicinal cream onto the affected areas, something she didn't appreciate. The cream is called Fuciderm (and is not pronounced the way you might hope), and thus far has made no difference either.

Feeling slightly unfaithful, I packed Aloe into a travel box and drove to a homeopathic vet near Sevenoaks to see if something herbal could cure her.

The patient, whose social skills with many of our other chickens are reminiscent of a switchblade-wielding skinhead, was so well behaved that the vet commented on her calmness. He poked, peered, tweaked, said "Hmm," tipped some tiny white pills into a medicine bottle, and told me to administer them twice a day.

Chickens are dim, but like most animals they have an unerring ability to spot and spit out anything medicinal, so I asked if the pills could be mixed in with Aloe's regular feed.

"It's not ideal," said the vet. "To get the maximum benefit, you need the pills to make contact with the bird's mucus membrane." A lovely image, I'm sure you'll agree, and one that would necessitate twice-daily capturings, the prising open of beaks, and determined pill postings.

Meanwhile, Aloe and Vera continued to produce eggs like a pair of machine guns. I commented to a chicken expert about this pair's near-hybrid-laying levels, to be told that Neras laid like hybrids because that's what they were. So, after I'd decided not to buy more birds of this sort, four of our flock of seven are hybrids after all.

Part 2

On the Road

CHAPTER

4

Good Afternoon, Tunbridge Wells

BOOKISH BEGINNINGS

The Royal Victoria Parade in Tunbridge Wells is one of those shopping precincts those of us who hate shopping know and loathe. It has everything you could possibly want to buy or look at and wish you could afford. At Christmas it is stuffed with tense, drawn (probably overdrawn), and almost certainly overwrought people. In short, it is a British shopping paradise.

As a confirmed shopaphobic, I'd never want to set foot in such a place, and would especially wish to avoid one on a busy Saturday (although, huge, impersonal shopping malls would come even higher on any sensible person's amputation list), yet here I was, or, more accurately, here we were, on a busy Saturday not long before Christmas.

I was in the company of Peeping Chicken, and we weren't in the Victoria Parade to buy things. We were here to sell.

Our destination was a branch of Ottakar's, the bookstore chain which was the third stop on a mini book-promoting tour that was gradually taking us to Tenterden, Maidstone, Tunbridge Wells, Greenwich, and Ashford, areas all closely associated with the literati, or at least places with bookshops that were prepared to have us.

In Tunbridge Wells this meant sitting in the entrance to a bookshop at a table piled with copies of your book, in the hope that people passing through on their way to the Vin Diesel biography will buy some of them, especially if you scribble something on the flyleaves.

When I'd suggested this, my publishers had been supportive but cautious, warning that these things can be like the flipside of one of those nightmarish dreams in which you find yourself in the buff in the middle of Piccadilly Circus. Instead, you sit feeling exposed and looking self-conscious as the world mills around you looking for the latest Harry Potter or *The Little Book of Celebrity Dog Turds*. You aren't a person; you're an obstacle that needs to be navigated around.

We'd managed to wring a little advance publicity out of this and the signing sessions that had already taken place with an e-mailed local-newspaper press release, topped with the infinitely recyclable and entirely shameless headline of HEN MANIA COMES TO ————.

So far, all the venues Peeping and I had visited were within thirty miles of where we lived, allowing us to play the "local author" card. Anybody working on a regional newspaper during a slow news week is likely to fall with a glad cry on a reasonably punctuated and concise news release about something new happening on their patch, especially when there's an OK, copyright-free photo with a cute-ish animal involved, so our bookshop travels had generated some column inches. We were ideal picture-caption material.

I'd also put some miles on the Google search engine, dug up the contact details of most of the local radio stations and pestered them, resulting in more over-the-phone question-and-answer sessions about the personalities, or otherwise, of our chickens, together with the inevitable inquiries about feeding on, rather than just feeding, our flock.

These things were immensely helpful, both in terms of telling people about the book and mentioning that the person who wrote it would be in their area desperately trying to peddle some copies.

To assist with the process, the bookshop crew at Tunbridge Wells had provided a table, a couple of chairs, and a worryingly large quantity of books for me to sign if hordes of customers turned up. If they didn't, hiding would be difficult, so I plonked Peeping's travel box on the table, said yes to the proffered cup of tea, and waited.

Peeping seemed indifferent to the comings and goings inside the average bookshop. As there was food and drink to be had in her travel case—which was a reasonably private space if she decided not to study the public as they hurtled from one retail activity to the next—she sat, shat, foraged, and preened.

She was rarely called upon to venture out of her box. When this happened it was generally so a child could feed her, or fail to feed her if the bird was feeling contrary. We'd also had a couple of local newspaper photographers and journalists come along to write follow-up stories.

CANDID CAMERAS

Local press photographers seem to have certain standard compositions they like to use. There's the up-the-nose shot of local dignitaries. How many mayors with bad teeth and chunky gold chains have discovered they had five extra chins as a result of this technique? Then there's the "heads-together, thumbs-up-with-charity-check" shot, in which a trio of bashful persons are scrunched together for accidental humiliation purposes. Local papers are also stuffed with pictures that "tell a story."

Then there are photos involving lots of people—a football team, say—where half of them get down on one knee while the others stand behind them. These are genuinely known in the trade as "firing squad" shots. There's certainly something of the firing squad about the lives of local newspaper photographers, as they hurtle from golden-wedding celebration ("Raise those glasses!") to school play to unsmiling mustached policeman with charity bike-riding colleagues to the guy with the chicken in the bookshop.

There isn't much time to explore the artistic side of photography, and, when you're confronted with a human being, a hen, a pile of books, and about ten minutes to do something with them compositionally, the answer seems to be to get the human being to pick up a book, stuff it next to the left side of his head, slightly angled, then lean forward so that the chicken he's hopefully persuaded to sit on his lap is level with his right ear. You then sprawl on the floor so that your subjects loom over you and passing shoppers nearly trip over your prone form.

Sometimes you tower over the subject, so his chicken becomes slightly alarmed. One guy with a more fully developed spatial awareness than some of his more pressed-for-time colleagues sat cross-legged in front of me and asked that I open my knees.

The photographer who came to Tunbridge Wells was unusual in that he was under fifty, but like his colleagues he was friendly and slightly harassed.

We had a brief negotiation over what Peeping and I might actually do, and after I demurred from the idea of a book-'n'-chicken-moon-faced-grinning-idiot job, we went for something along the lines of "man with chicken on his lap pretends he's reading to it." We also had a little go at putting some raisins on the pile of books to get Peeping looking (or "peeping"?) in their general direction.

She thought this was a good idea, and began demolishing her raisin supply while in the process putting tiny, beak-shaped dents in the book covers, something I selfishly chose not to mention as I scooped the bird's treats onto the table and off the books.

At this stage a reporter appeared. Like most local newspaper reporters I've met, this person was brisk, polished, aged about twenty-three, female, and wanted to know whether our chickens had individual personalities and if we ate them.

I leered and mumbled, Peeping pecked, and everyone got through this encounter unscathed.

PEEPING'S PUBLIC

In the meantime customers had begun arriving. "Oh look, it's a chicken!" became a familiar cry of parents anxious to find a way of preventing their tiny charges from yanking the books from the shelves.

In between introducing Peeping to her school-aged public ("Would you like to feed her? No, it won't hurt if she pecks at the food in your hand. She's done a poo—isn't that funny?" etc.), mostly chicken-keeping grown-ups arrived and asked questions about breeds and ailments, which indicated that many of them knew much more than I did.

Two visitors stuck in my mind. The first was a fifty-something mother and her grown-up daughter, who stopped and chatted for quite some time. The mother had seen us on television.

"I've been on morning TV as well," she said.

"Oh, really, why's that?"

"It was an item about recovering heroin addicts. I was one of the mothers," she said brightly, as if she'd been talking about flower arranging.

Later, another lady appeared with her husband. She was clasping a cat box of her own, in which sat a handsome, if mildly perplexed-looking, hen.

"Where are the other chickens?" asked its owner, in a tone of genuine surprise. She'd expected the bookshop to be filled with birds

and their keepers. By this stage Peeping was back in her travel box, so the two birds peered at each other from behind bars. It was obvious that neither wanted to make friends.

In book-selling terms, the day proved a success. We found homes for about fifty copies, and departed with a certain glow.

A visit to Waterstone's in the throbbing metropolis of Maidstone was a rather lower-key affair. Peeping and I spent the best part of a day sitting behind a desk staring into the middle distance. The longest conversation we had was with a polite but angry lady who said taking a chicken to a bookshop was "a cheap stunt."

She wasn't among the fourteen people who bought books, but this shop visit represented the publishing hall of plenty compared with our plans to visit bookshops in High Wycombe and Windsor. The idea of going to these venues had a certain slightly daft appeal, as they're both centers of provincial theater where you can see down-on-their-luck ex-TV stars on stage.

Then there are the pantomine plays. Would Windsor and High Wycombe be the same places without an annual invasion of grease-painted, thigh-slapping newscasters and hard-up ex-Australian TV soap stars? I think not. Anyway, the fiction of following in their sequined footsteps had a certain appeal.

The idea was that we'd do an evening program and actually talk about the book—OK, I'd talk about the book; Peeping would just cluck. But we didn't make it. Thanks to a blanket lack of interest we were canceled.

We very nearly failed in Lymington, which is a bloody long way from Kent. Five people turned up. A couple with two utterly bored small boys who entertained themselves by energetically whizzing around the bookshop, and a lady who wanted to keep chickens but didn't know where to start, or even where to find them. It turned out

the couple were hen experts with a big, entirely free-range flock. Addresses were exchanged and promises of help made. It was heartening, and very nearly made the 350-odd-mile trip worthwhile.

CAFÉ SOCIETY

It was just a few days before Christmas when Peeping and I undertook the last gig of this particular tour at a large bookshop hidden in the bowels of yet another shopping center. This one lurked somewhere up the back passage of Ashford, Kent.

If you want a socioeconomic snapshot of different parts of Britain, spend time in a few bookshops in different locations and you'll see a microcosm of human life passing through them.

The more prosperous places have book-selling venues with a certain shininess to them and people who are as likely to be browsing for something by Louis de Bernières as they are for a new copy of *Lemony Snicket*. Other bookshops, in places where, frankly, there's less cash, often have a wearier patina, and their clientele seem more careworn as they seek out the latest blockbuster novels by John Grisham and Danielle Steel.

Ashford isn't a desperate hellhole—far from it—but parts of it have an almost studied lack of *joie de vivre*. On a drizzle-marinated Saturday afternoon, if you're an adolescent with nothing to do, this must be pretty oppressive.

So a bookshop with a café is always going to be a magnet for teenagers, especially if boredom, nasty weather, and lack of cash are the driving forces behind visiting the place. It's amazing how long ten lugubrious-looking adolescents can linger over three cups of curdling coffee.

In the average fast-food outlet they'd be given the evil eye for hanging around and taking valuable table space that could otherwise go to families intent on buying lard-and-asbestos burgers with

French fries made from real compressed sawdust. In bookshops, hanging around is positively encouraged—it's called browsing.

Peeping and I had set up our stall next to this particular book-shop's café, and it must be said that trade was slow. I did that staring self-consciously thing as Peeping ate and tore at the newspaper that lined her travel box. We were, however, perfectly placed to provide entertainment for the damp knots of teenagers who were about twenty feet away, huddled or sprawled as they contemplated a few cups of coffee. This was browsing without the inconvenience of read-ing any of the books.

They saw a man with silly hair and a chicken in a cat box. I saw hard-faced girls with hooded jackets in pale Barbie pinks and blues, lapels fuzzy with the sort of fake fur that only a mechanical animal could have produced. Lips were glossed with what looked like shiny industrial lacquer; flared trousers flapped heavily over clunky shoes,

especially those whose bottoms had been trailed along rain-lashed pavements, soaking up discolored water as their owners tottered or flounced toward another Saturday in downtown Ashford.

The boys also wore jackets with hoods, many of which remained firmly pulled over small angular heads, balanced on the ends of long necks. Perhaps the hoods were partially glued in situ by the hair gel favored by many of their owners, some of whom seemed to have had their hair teased and styled into fake comb-overs. In a few years some of them would have the real thing.

The hooded look may be the height of shopping-center chic if you're sixteen, but to an old fart like me the end result resembled a convention of junior Grim Reapers with only bony fingers, triangular Adam's apples, chins, big noses, and zits sticking out of their mall clothes to prove their humanity.

Yet teenagers haven't changed much in the million years since I stopped being one. Adults still go on about how awful it is to be adolescent, when most of the time you feel exactly the same as you always did. Decrepit people go on about how teenagers mumble incomprehensibly and/or inarticulately, yet all your peers make perfect sense to you. The most innocent remark can result in raised voices and accusations of rudeness and ungraciousness from adults, and the word "no" seems to be applied to every request you make. Meanwhile, a large proportion of your life involves just waiting for something exciting to happen.

The wider world of human dinosaurs, populated by people of your parents' and grandparents' generations, regard you as a distraction, a worry, an irritant, or vaguely threatening. The last can be quite fun, once you've discovered which buttons to press to wind up adults who have no real sanctions over you.

As someone who has virtually nothing to do with teenagers and, unless I'm concentrating very hard, an unfortunate habit of lapsing

into a sort of patronizing "grown-up speak" when I do, I feel slightly vulnerable to being wound up. I'd never make a good teacher.

Worse, I did feel threatened. I knew this was irrational, but, for the sake of the chicken, hoped I could hide this.

THE PENGUIN

Peeping and I started to become something of an attraction when one boy who'd bucked the dress code by pulling down his hood spied us from the other side of the shop. His mouth fell open.

"Oi! It's a penguin!" he shouted, pointing at Peeping, who was peering out through the open lid of her box. "What's a penguin doin' in a bookshop?"

If there was irony to this question, he hid it well. I really don't think he knew what he was looking at. When Peeping's origins were explained he said, "Right," imbuing the word with a tone that screamed, "I am not impressed." Then he asked, "So what's a *chicken* doing in a bookshop?"

Two moon-faced, thirteen-year-oldish boys, both pale and chunky—no, let's be truthful here: "lumpy" is a better word—sidled over and scrutinized Peeping, who stopped eating and regarded them back.

"My grandpa's got chickens," said the shorter, rounder member of the duo, "but we're not allowed to keep them."

I asked where he lived. The boy named a neighborhood well known to locals for its low-level social deprivation and worn-down ugliness. People who don't live there make judgments about people who do. I tried not to, and was soon locked into one of those conversations in which you're asked questions that are absolutely direct yet impossible to answer, along the lines of, "Why isn't your chicken laying an egg now?" or "Why isn't it a boy?" There was no facetiousness intended in what was being asked. The questions were the thirteen-year-old's equivalent of conversational filler, a way to bridge a rather obvious gap of mutual awkwardness.

I quickly gave up trying to offer meaningful answers. The lumpy duo were doing their best, but neither was skilled at concealing boredom, and I was soon aware that the stuff I was saying was being turned from recognizable words into a low-pitched droning noise from the time it left my mouth to when it reached their ears.

Feet were shuffled, eyes rolled, and brows furrowed, so I asked if they'd like to feed Peeping, and an altogether different look was exchanged between the two. A look that might almost have been excitement.

There was a pause.

"Er—no, that's all right," said the smaller one, who was clearly the spokesman. He sounded a little wistful.

"Are you sure?"

"No. Thanks, though."

They moved away, then hovered around some bookshelves where they could keep Peeping under observation.

The vacuum they left wasn't filled with reassuring grown-ups. Instead, a bigger group of older teens started to take an interest in us. They'd been huddled around their coffee cups for so long that not only would an impermeable membrane of skin have formed on their contents, but a nice culture of mold would have taken hold on top of that.

There were about ten boys and girls with brittle voices and streetwise mannerisms. To me they looked tough and alien.

"Can we come and see your chicken?"

"What's it called?"

"Why's it called that?"

"Peeping? Yeah, right."

I sat on the table next to Peeping's box as they crowded around. I wondered whether this would frighten the bird, but they didn't actually loom over her. It occurred to me that this might well have been the closest many of them had ever been to a chicken, and perhaps *they* were nervous of *her*.

"Can I feed it?" asked a girl.

I tipped some raisins into one her small upturned hands, noticing the giant white nail extensions.

The food was tentatively offered, and when Peeping struck, the hand was jerked away again.

"Is it going to hurt?" asked the girl.

I promised it wouldn't.

"But its nose looks sharp."

"Beak!" said someone disdainfully. "It's called a beak."

"Beak, then."

Peeping was entirely happy with the arrangement, and it wasn't long before a cheerful, disorderly line had more or less formed itself. Food was tipped from hand to hand as aspirant hard nuts and their amours took turns feeding the chicken. This was an activity that took about five years off each participant's age. Under carefully hard-boiled exteriors children could be seen having a good time.

"Are you a celebrity?" said a voice from inside one of the hoods. What was actually said came out as a single word: "Youslebrity?" The rough translation of this presumably is, "Are you on TV?" I said No, I wasn't, and hoped the questioner wasn't disappointed.

OF PEEPING AND PENISES

There were some attempts at stroking Peeping. She was less keen on this, but showed active displeasure only when one of the girls tried stroking her feathers in the wrong direction.

"Ooo, sorry," she tittered.

Somebody asked if chickens could "make babies on their own."

"Does it have a penis?" asked one of the boys.

I said something to the effect that Peeping was female, and that you needed a male chicken to produce chicks. This led to further "Well, that's bloody obvious to me" harrumphings from other members of the line, but it wasn't long before avian wedding tackle was back on the conversation agenda.

"Do their penises fall off?" asked another hooded comic.

"That depends," I said.

"So in the morning, do you have to pick up all the penises that have fallen off?" persisted the hooded one, before cackling like a machine gun.

"Not lately," I said, trying to deadpan the conversation without appearing shocked—which I wasn't—or tediously sanctimonious ("That isn't very funny, is it, sonny?").

Eventually, two or three more teens arrived to lure their chicken-petting friends onto Ashford's wet, meanish streets. By then this group had ceased to be a generic blob or gang that in all honesty I might have tried reasonably hard to avoid. They'd become semi-innocent individuals, hiding behind half-knowing, half-bullshitting exteriors.

They were gentle with Peeping, and operated as a sort of pack, egging each other on with a mix of bravado and naiveté. There was nothing malicious about them, although under different circumstances I could see us not getting on so well.

"See you, mate!" said the penis humorist as they finally clattered away.

Peeping and I weren't alone for long. Within minutes the two younger boys who'd eschewed chicken-feeding were back. If it was an OK activity for a bunch of fifteen- to sixteen-year-olds, then it was all right for them.

The pair stayed for over twenty minutes, swapping places to tickle and feed. Peeping, who by then must have weighed the chicken equivalent of 250 pounds, obliged them both by eating copiously.

The one who did more of the talking seemed lost in thought. Then he said, "When I grow up I'm going to keep chickens." Pondering a utopian, adult future, this teenaged rebel added, "And nobody's going to stop me."

5

Gone West
(and East)

STRICTLY WITH THE BIRDS

When I next took to the road, it wasn't with Peeping Chicken. There'd been a natural hiatus during which she'd got on with being a chicken, living with other chickens rather than spending extended periods of time with me.

The last outing we'd shared had been to the Woodchurch village men's group, which involved extended exposure to some good-natured gents who were mostly of retirement age, some of whom kept chickens, and once again knew more about the subject's minutiae than I did.

Peeping had taken this encounter in her stride, but several weeks later, when I was asked to talk about chickens and writing at a bookshop in Peterfield, she was more than reluctant to be caught. Once imprisoned in her cat box, the bird scuttled about, head jerking from side to side. She wanted to get out.

Hoping she'd become calmer, I packed the car and set out, but five miles into the journey she was still very active, panting hard and obviously stressed. I turned around, headed for home, and swapped the unhappy creature for Vera the Nera, who was completely calm—calmer than I was, since we were now running late. We hurtled to the venue and walked through the door exactly when we were due to start. I began speaking as we staggered into view and had to bluff my way through the entire encounter.

Since then Peeping has regained her equilibrium and retains the title of our flock's friendliest bird, who thoroughly enjoys being fussed over and is happy to eat out of our hands, but her traveling days are over.

When Vera isn't on duty, my traveling companion is the venerable Tikka. If anything, she's even calmer than Vera, and has been from King's Lynn to Aberystwyth.

For the King's Lynn trip my wife Jane came too. This was just as well, as on the morning we were due to set off, I decided to clean

and refill the big galvanized water container used by the birds who were staying behind. This is a hefty item, made heftier still when several gallons of water is added to it.

I picked it up in a silly way and felt an unpleasant mangled-vertebrae sensation about three-quarters of the way down my spine. Foolishly, I still tottered up the garden clasping the sodding waterer, and by the time I'd gotten back to the house I was grimacing, hobbling and S-shaped.

I couldn't even pick up a pencil case without cursing, so Jane loaded the car and did most of the driving. King's Lynn is a long way from Kent, and when we arrived at the bed-and-breakfast my spine had completely seized up. Unseizing it hurt like hell, and, being a real man, I shared my discomfort with Jane and Tikka.

If the pain and walking about like a ramrod did not improve my temper, the bed-and-breakfast brought on a psychotic twitch. It had been selected from a book of such places that "welcomed" pets. On the phone I'd told a cheerful-sounding woman with a grandmotherly voice that we would be coming as a threesome, and that although Tikka wouldn't be joining us in the bedroom, a quiet parking lot was required so that her portable residence would be reasonably noise-free.

Grandma extolled the virtues of the parking lot, which turned out to be a former front garden covered in pebbles and crowded with the cars of other guests. There was a curb that led directly onto an extremely busy arterial road along which trucks, buses, and a thousand sales reps rumbled.

In a hallway wallpapered with mauve flowers that somehow spewed forth, we were greeted by a small, severe-looking, elderly lady who demanded exorbitant payment in advance, just in case we ran away in the small hours.

We were lucky, she said. Our room had an en suite shower.

Actually, the room itself was the size of an en suite shower. It was cramped, narrow, and gloomy, but naturally featured its own psychedelic wallpaper and a revolting photo of modern stage school moppets dressed as Depression-era waifs. The duvet had a plant motif and was lightly stained, although the stains did appear to have been recently washed.

Attempts at opening the plastic replacement windows revealed a remarkable strain of East Anglian mold, which adhered doggedly to the polymer window frames and plastic sealant rather than plaster, brick, or paint.

As for that en suite shower, this was half of a built-in wardrobe and resembled a dwarf's telephone booth with a clear glass door that banged against the end of the bed when opened. There was no shower curtain. The space to its left had been given over to a slightly crooked toilet and a dentist's spitting bowl masquerading as a sink. This did have a door—one of those fake wood-effect plastic folding jobs, against which your knees get jammed when you're using the toilet.

Would it surprise you to discover that the mattress had suffered nervous collapse? It was like sleeping on a giant marshmallow that had been battered to death, and my back suffered accordingly.

The following morning it took ten minutes of grimacing and moaning before I managed to get dressed. Jane had to put on my shoes before I hobbled down to an entirely cheerless breakfast that was clearly overfamiliar with the inside of a microwave oven.

The only B&B I've stayed in that managed to be less enticing was an establishment on the outer reaches of Norwich. Painted blood red, it welcomed you with a cobweb-covered security camera, a cross-looking Alsatian dog, and damp beds.

The place was also run by an old lady. At breakfast I had had the temerity to ask her for a second piece of flinty bacon. Watery eyes

were rolled before she shuffled into the kitchen, returning with the requested piece of pig on a plate, which she slammed down in front of me, uttering the immortal words, "There you go, Oliver Twist!"

We haven't been back.

The center of King's Lynn is actually very attractive, even if it is used as a huge parking lot. I was in too much pain to appreciate this as Jane levered me out of the car, managing not to say, "It's only a sore back—for Christ's sake, stop moaning."

I felt two inches shorter than normal and walked very slowly, both hands outstretched like a slightly deformed Wild West gun-slinger. Jane carried Tikka in her box as I hobbled along a few yards behind her. We were nearly at the bookshop when we came across an animal rights protest connected to duck farming.

I know, a chicken is not a duck, nobody was going to eat this one, and she had actually been liberated from a farm, but I somehow felt explanations might be tricky. Selfishly, I wished very strongly to be somewhere else, but sensed that any attempts at moving faster would result in a nasty rupture somewhere.

Why we weren't noticed I'll never know, but we made it to the bookstore. I was plonked onto a chair and Jane, who had suffered enough, told me that she was anxious to explore the delights of King's Lynn, and that Tikka and I would have to make our own entertainment.

Ever since that day I've approached the chicken waterer with a new respect.

BACK ON THE ROAD

My back had long since healed when Tikka was next called on to meet her adoring public, but, probably as a consequence of all the deathbed stuff described earlier, I'd become very run-down and contracted a delightful infection. Curing it involved drinking lots of water and taking a course of antibiotics that could knock an elephant onto its ass.

Tikka and I had an itinerary that would take us from Kent to Hampshire, where we'd swap cars, then make our way to Gloucester, Carmarthen, and Aberystwyth. I realized that prodigious fluid intake would result in regular pit stops, but it had to be done.

As a freelance journalist specializing in cars, I write for a magazine rejoicing in the title of *4x4 and MPV Driver*. The editor, Bob Murray, is a bit of a lateral thinker, and had e-mailed all his contributing writers asking if they had any holiday or travel plans that could involve using a shiny new press car, and which would make a series of linked stories.

He liked the idea of something on a book tour involving a live chicken—well, wouldn't you?—and said he could even supply the car, which was a Renault Megane Grand Scenic.

I'd spread newspaper on the front passenger seat and put Tikka's travel box on top of that, securing her with a seat belt ("If you get chicken shit in this, there'll be trouble," Bob had said). As we called in at a supermarket to buy enough bottled water to fill the average bath, I became aware that I was developing a headache. More specifically, it started to feel as if a small, determined hand was squeezing my left eyeball.

Squinting slightly at Tikka and the other highway drivers, I headed for Gloucester and the first of a series of bed-and-breakfasts with quiet parking lots that in a fit of organizational zeal I'd pre-booked.

The miles rolled by. Tikka and I ignored each other as the eyeball discomfort spread to the left side of my head and my eyelid started to twitch. When indigestion set in I crawled off the highway, found a side road in an industrial complex, parked, and fell into a very deep sleep that lasted for a couple of hours, waking to a bladder that felt like a blimp (I'd been studious about my fluid intake) and the sound of clucking and scuffling from the cat box. Tikka appeared to be laying an egg.

After a desperate dash to find a bathroom, I felt a bit wobbly but generally better, so we pressed on to Gloucester and the B&B. This was a big, attractive-looking Edwardian townhouse that had been "modernized" inside with ruthless ineptitude around 1974. After changing Tikka's bedding I offered her some extra raisins for the inconvenience, signed in, and was shown to my room, a high-ceilinged cell painted a violent neon orange. Never mind—it was clean, the bath was big, and I planned to spend most of my time in

the bedroom with the lights off and my eyes shut, so the decor didn't matter.

A present from Egypt

Later, Tikka and I did one of our two-handed bookshop events to a gratifyingly large, friendly audience, including a small child who had a go at undoing my shoelaces. Having said our good-byes, Tikka polished off some sweet corn and I found an Italian restaurant where I demolished a valedictory pizza. The place seemed awfully hot, and by the time I left I was perspiring attractively.

Outside, the world felt unpleasantly cold and I started to shiver. In bed at the B&B things quickly heated up again, and I was soon simmering. It felt as if I were glowing in sympathy with the room's color scheme. Then it dawned. Less than a week before, Jane and I had returned from a holiday to Egypt, smugly congratulating ourselves on evading the various travelers' bugs that the guidebooks describe with lugubrious detail. Clearly I hadn't, and was now traveling with a chicken, fragile waterworks, and a Middle Eastern holiday memento.

What a disaster! I'm not good at being ill, and I spent hours dozing fitfully, cursing, leaking from every pore, and tottering to the bathroom to drink gallons of water. Alone in this cliché of a traveling salesman's bedchamber I found it easy to feel cooked, miserable, and singular. My wife was cosseted in the marital bed 150 miles away, so could not be prevailed upon to be endlessly sorry for me as I made the duvet unbearably hot and perhaps gave it my bug. It was all so unfair.

I lay in the dark and considered all the negatives. There were plenty to choose from. I still had hundreds of miles to drive in a strange car on roads I didn't know, and would be forced to stay in lonely places just like this one. I'd have to be nice to people and make entertaining conversation when I felt like shit, and when I wasn't doing that the only company I'd have would be a chicken.

Slithering in a slick of sweat and self-pity, I eventually fell into a deeper, super-heated sleep and woke the following morning feeling completely fine. A light-brown headache, which quickly vanished, and attractively damp bedsheets were the only remnants of a red-hot night. Presumably, whatever had been bothering me had been expunged along with the fifteen gallons of water I'd consumed.

Later, sprawling in the room's enormous bath, I realized that I was both a miserable bore and a lucky sod, and, having dressed, then dined greedily and greasily on the B&B's extensive cooked breakfast, headed for Wales, having first given Tikka the toast I'd pinched for the purpose.

A WELSH ABER-RATION

We were some way over the Welsh border, heading for Carmarthen and trickling happily along the highway when a vague sense of ill ease took on a more specific, unpleasant form. The following day we were due in Aberystwyth, but it looked as if I'd booked a bed-and-breakfast in Abergavenny by mistake. Aberystwyth is a coastal town by the Irish Sea, whereas Abergavenny is not so very far from the Bristol Channel. They're both in Wales and have names beginning with *Aber*, but the distance between them is huge.

I stopped the car, rang the B&B and quickly had my worst suspicions confirmed.

"Sorry, pal. We're nowhere near Aberystwyth," said a cheerful voice. I groveled, canceled, and then made arrangements that meant Tikka and I wouldn't both be sleeping in an RV up an Aberystwyth side street the following night. My brain clearly hadn't been functioning properly for some time. This had been a very lucky escape.

It was mid-afternoon when we reached Carmarthen to find that large swathes of the roads were being dug up. We sat in traffic jams, then managed to get lost, but at least the sun was shining, and Tikka

had laid another egg somewhere near a place called Llanspyddid. However, the niggling ill ease had returned.

I stopped and consulted my scribbled list of bed-and-breakfasts. Had I canceled tonight's accommodation in Carmarthen by accident? I certainly hadn't asked the B&B's location when I'd phoned.

"Yes?" said the still-friendly voice when I phoned again. "We're in Carmarthen, which as I said is a long way from Aberystwyth. And you canceled, right? I remember you because you're the guy with the chicken."

Fortunately, the room was still available. I un-canceled, did the telephone equivalent of groveling, and then phoned the "right" wrong B&B, groveled again, and set off once more in search of the place I was actually supposed to be staying in.

This was "around the corner from where you are, off the high street—sharp left, under an arch," which sounded simple enough to find. This was gratifying, since I'd been at the mineral water again and was looking forward to meeting up with this particular establishment's facilities.

Twenty minutes later I was *really* looking forward to this encounter. Carmarthen's main shopping street is narrow and cluttered. Progress had been completely blocked by a delivery truck. All I could do was look wistfully at the B&B entrance less than fifty yards ahead.

This was an archway between two shops, and when I finally got to it the thing seemed to shrink. Now this shouldn't be a problem to a driving expert, should it? Even a flustered one desperate for a pee.

I proceeded with care, concentrating on keeping the front bumper from connecting with the archway's stucco right-hand wall. We crept forward. The car gently swung around. Then came the awful crunching noise as the Renault's left-hand rear flank bit into the opposite wall.

Mortified, I began swearing, which at least drowned out the further inevitable grinding noises as I reversed out again and embedded the passenger-side door mirror into the stucco. As it connected, the mirror's plastic cover made a loud cracking noise, which echoed in the archway. This alerted the guy I'd spoken to on the phone. By the time he reached us I was out of the car, on a Carmarthen street, cursing and dancing up and down with embarrassed rage.

I wanted to pee, I wanted to be somewhere else, and I wanted, very, very much, for this not to have happened.

To his credit, the B&B person, who was about eighteen, managed not to laugh.

"I think I'd better park it for you, sir," he said, climbing into the driver's seat, glancing briefly at Tikka, then expertly negotiating the car through that bastard of an arch and into the courtyard beyond, leaving the professional driving expert to trudge along in his wake.

A SENSE OF RELIEF—TIMES TWO

With added stretch marks, this particular Grand Scenic was both less grand and less scenic than before, but luckily the damage was minor and mostly cosmetic. However, I still felt like a bloody fool. Having relieved myself in the physical sense, I took a deep breath and got on the phone for further groveling. The folks at Renault were very nice about the assault inflicted on their car, and so was Bob, which, given that the thing had been lent to him as a long-term test vehicle, was just as well.

Having changed Tikka's water and given her fresh food and new bedding, I tottered up to my room, shoved a pillow over my eyes, and headed for blissful unconsciousness. Later, when Tikka and I arrived at the venue where we'd been booked to visit, everybody was very understanding about having to hang around for about twenty minutes because I'd written down the wrong arrival time.

That night I dined alone on plastic fish and chips in a plastic theme pub where robotic staff spent the entire time sidling up to my table and asking, "Is everything OK?" I smiled and said "yes" over and over again, which in the wider sense was a lie, although I fervently hoped that it might, eventually, be true.

6

Redemption

THERE WAS A CROOKED HOUSE

When we reached Aberystwyth the next afternoon things had improved. I hadn't gotten lost or bashed the car into any solid objects. We'd found the place we were staying in, and it was a proper hotel, although the proprietor here seemed to have a thing about orange as a color scheme, too, since this was the color he'd chosen for the awnings of his empire, which was actually a trio of tall, good-looking, elderly buildings that had been knocked together.

The place was absolutely labyrinthine, and I spent a great deal of time getting lost, wheezing up and down flights of stairs, ending up in a restaurant or back at the reception area before finally reaching my room, an immaculate, cozy annex tucked away in what could almost be called the "west wing."

It felt good to be in the right place at the right time, although there was something slightly disorienting about my room. It took a few minutes to work out why this was: all the walls sloped at different angles; the door and door frame seemed slightly off-kilter too; ditto the sash window. There was also a definite slope to the floor.

Still, the room was spotless, not painted orange, and even had a computer jack plug, which was useful, since as a freelance journalist I still had a living to earn and had brought my word processor along as I needed to file a story by e-mail.

Although I use a computer for work, my understanding of how the thing does its stuff is basic at best. I'm like the person who can drive a car, but has no idea what goes on under the hood. This is fine until something goes wrong, then I'm screwed, to use a technical term. The fact that most of the people who fix these things speak technodrivel rather than English doesn't help, either.

My dad, who is a good ten years beyond retirement age, loves computers, understands their little ways, and is entirely up to speed with all the latest developments. When my computer freezes, so do I.

He, instead, takes his apart. This generational about-face element to our relationship is useful to me, because I can still phone him up and say, "Dad, it doesn't work."

However, this time I couldn't, because he was out, so I spoke to the hotel receptionist, who couldn't understand why there was a problem, since they'd just had broadband installed. She'd get the proprietor to come to my room and sort it out.

The man who appeared at my door was middle-aged, short, and stocky, and moved in a way that indefinably marked him out as an ex-soldier. His luxuriant mustache resembled two well-fed black caterpillars, and he wore a baseball cap with aspirations to join the headgear equivalent of the army.

He was immensely friendly, chatty, and keen to help, but it was obvious that he was also even more of a computer illiterate than I was. Unlike me, he had a puppyish enthusiasm for pressing ahead anyway and the sort of self-belief that always results in fruitlessly pressing keys and dialing numbers, "because we've just had broadband installed, you know. It's the latest thing. You just try X. It'll work this time. Oh, well, never mind. You're not doing it right. What you need to do is . . ."

The irritation I felt was mixed with guilt. The man was being so kind. I just wanted to find an Internet café and send my story from there, but he wouldn't hear of it. "We've got broadband, you know . . ."

In the end we decanted the thing I'd written onto a floppy disk and once again headed for reception. "We'll send it from there," said The Proprietor.

On the way down I asked him about the building's lopsidedness. "Subsidence. But don't worry. It was twenty years ago. It's been fixed now."

Why was I in town with a chicken? he asked.

"I'm promoting a book."

"You're an author?" said The Proprietor, his voice rising with excitement. I knew what was coming next.

"I'm writing a little book. Could you offer me some advice on getting it published?"

In the narrow lobby, which petered out under a staircase, he swapped places with the rather demure receptionist, planted himself squarely in front of a computer terminal, and launched into the electronic unknown.

"Is it this one?" he asked as icons and graphics came and went. "We've had this professionally installed, it's . . ."

Eventually he and the receptionist changed places yet again, and with a few keystrokes she'd tracked down the right site and the thing I'd been trying to send for the past hour successfully hurtled down a phone line from Aberystwyth to a publishing house in exotic, distant Peterborough.

THE SOLDIER'S TALE

"Let me tell you about my book," said The Proprietor. "It's about my life."

What followed was a roller-coaster story. Our man had left Aberystwyth as a raw army recruit and seen action in the Falklands. Afterwards there'd been a career as a top-flight chef, working with the Roux brothers; but a liking for easily accessible alcohol led to a spiraling drink problem, an imploding career, family problems, and a miserable life running a provincial café.

There'd been a personal reckoning, during which he'd come back to Aberystwyth and started again. He'd been dry for years, and this hotel, with a restaurant where he practiced his cooking skills, was the result.

He wasn't very good at sending e-mails, but so what?

While all this was going on Tikka was rather missing out on quality time. Taking her for a walk in the middle of Aberystwyth wasn't really an option, and there wasn't a penned area for her to scratch about and forage in, so, before an evening of yet more book-plugging got under way, I sat in the car, planted her on my news-paper-covered lap, and proffered some edible treats intended to make the process of traveling and meeting the public less of a bore.

She'd developed a particular liking for wild birdseed with peanuts. This is expensive stuff, but offering it seemed the least I could do. I persuaded her to sit by stroking and tickling her back, then offered a handful of food, which she seemed to enjoy.

True, she would much rather have been out and about with her own kind, but she was by then less than a day away from going home and doing just that. Spending time with an animal that, if nothing else, is prepared to view you as a "least bad" option rather than a threat or something to be feared has a certain attraction, even if that animal is a chicken. I was just glad that nobody could see us.

The other reason for these encounters was to calm the bird before she was put in the unnatural situation of being surrounded by a lot of people, some of whom might be keen to make her closer acquaintance. Indeed, a chicken-keeping lady in Carmarthen had made such a fuss of Tikka that the pair had ended up being photographed together, the bird firmly and expertly clasped to her admirer's breast for the purpose.

HUMAN HENS GO PARTYING

Our appearance at the Aberystwyth branch of Ottakar's did not re-quire similar fortitude on Tikka's part (although she genuinely didn't seem to mind the attention), but when Inge, the manager, asked if I'd like to go to the pub, it was decided that the bird could stay behind with the rest of her supper, which she'd more than earned.

"You can collect her on the way home," said Inge.

Although Tikka was staying behind, Inge and I were to be joined by a member of the audience, a Welsh-language book publisher who, I'm glad to say, was called Dylan.

Dylan had asked some esoteric yet comic questions about man's relationship with chickens ("How can you tell when they're happy?") and vice versa, and on the way to the pub revealed himself to be one of those quiet people who are almost permanently funny.

If Dylan was funny, the pub was positively hilarious. Tucked up a side street, it was doing a brisk trade for a chilly Thursday night.

At the bar were a group of lightly paint- and plaster-spattered guys who seemed intent on having a good time downing pints of freezing lager. In another corner was a sort of hen party of eighteen- to twenty-year-old girls who'd clearly been at the sauce for a long time. There was no doubt that they were (a) drunk and (b) having a

very good time indeed. They wore big smiles and tight clothes that clung to mostly ample figures that might have been described as Mc-Donald's Pre-Raphaelite.

Someone from this party had been feeding the jukebox a second mortgage's worth of coins, and that someone clearly had a fetish for 1980s pop. This seemed a bit weird, since most of the girls would barely have been out of diapers when the songs they'd chosen were current. No matter. They knew the words, and a massed impromptu karaoke session had developed. Imagine one of Lionel Richie's more glutinous offerings being pulverized by the vocal cords of an enthusiastic women's rugby team and you've pretty much grasped what we could hear.

The pub's interior was divided by old-fashioned, fixed wooden screens with bench seats attached to these and the walls. It wasn't long before some of the girls were dancing on the benches in a sort of fuddled, big-booted cancan.

"Tay-ke on meeeeee!" they bellowed when an ancient A-Ha song attempted to escape from the jukebox. No chance. The girls soon had it cornered and resistance was useless. This was the musical equivalent of hunting with hounds.

"*Tay-ke on me-eee-eee-eeeeeeeeeeee!!!!*" they chorused as the original collapsed under a flailing mass of tonsils.

At some point the massed ranks of painters and decorators decided to offer their considered opinion of the girls' singing talents. As one they turned from the bar, dropped their trousers, and mooned the hen party, who joyously went "Aaaaaaagh!"

Dylan and I made for the bar. As we waited one of the girls half shimmied, half staggered toward us. Dressed entirely in black, she looked vaguely like a goth with a knitted top, and was happily plastered—if not by the plasterers. Having invaded my personal space, she more or less stopped, the lager-relaxed pupils of her eyes studied my hairline, and then she produced a small purple sticker and slapped it

onto my head. Words were written on the sticker. They said, FUNKY FRIEND.

What a lovely gift. The giver was clearly intent on saying something, but was first having to deal with the conflicting demands on her of breathing, focusing, and standing up. I waited as the mental impulses that would allow her to do so marshalled themselves. Then she spoke.

"You remind me of my friend, you do . . ."

"Do I?"

"Yes," she hissed. "When he's old."

It could have been worse. She might have told me that I looked like her dad "when he's old."

As Dylan and I carried the drinks back we were pursued by a rising sense of hysteria—the sort that makes everything seem funny. I

had come all the way from Kent to Wales, piddling like a fire hydrant as I went, had crashed someone else's new car, heard the life story of a reformed-alcoholic soldier/chef, and been told by a tanked Aberystwyth teenager that I looked like her friend "when he's old." And I had made this journey with a live chicken. Suddenly it all seemed worthwhile, and would, I knew, make great copy. Even my inner cynic was happy.

It still seemed worthwhile when the three of us tipped into an Indian restaurant and ended up talking about cars, hens, moving from England to Wales, and comparative religion—the staff joined in on the last topic.

The happy glow was still in place the next morning as I prepared to drive home and said good-bye to the hotelier. Still wearing that hat, he was affability itself, despite the belt filled with enormous bullets, the camouflage jacket, and shotgun slung over his shoulder.

"Geese," he explained. "When the train takes you out of Aberystwyth, it goes over a bridge with some marshes at the bottom. That's where there's a club for people to shoot the geese. It's a bit exclusive. When I left I looked down on those marshes and said to myself, 'One day, when I come back, I'll shoot those geese myself.' And now," he said with a happy smile, "I do. You look after that chicken now!"

We shook hands, the bones of my right hand being compressed in the inevitable crunching grip.

In the car I gave Tikka her breakfast and set off for home, wondering why I'd found this goose-stalking hotelier to be so likeable. On the surface we didn't have much in common, but I could appreciate his enthusiasm for life, even if many of the things that enthused him weren't exactly my cup of tea. And he'd been kind and welcoming, blunting the slightly isolating edge of being a long way from home, living an itinerant bed-and-breakfast existence.

I'd enjoyed meeting him, enjoyed meeting the people who'd come to see Tikka, and I'd enjoyed that pub. The idea of returning to Aberystwyth with Jane, but without the chicken, was an appealing one, and if we did I knew where we'd stay.

About an hour into the journey two things put a stop to these musings. Noises from the cat box indicated that another egg was on the way, and I became aware of an urgent need to find a loo. Life was getting back to normal.

Part 3

Further
Travels

7

Child's Play

MUTANTS OF A FEATHER . . .

One conceit I had with this book was to visit an inner-city school with a chicken to meet pupils who might never have seen one of these birds in the flesh (or feather), in the process dispensing an educationally useful, life-enhancing experience. Easy.

This was complacent and smug. Life is rather more complicated, which I was about to discover as I made my way through Blackheath to talk to a group of preschool children aged between eighteen months and four years.

My destination was the Lingfield Day Nursery. Tucked away in a leafy street of big, handsome town houses, it didn't have a lot to do with harsh, inner-city life, but that didn't mean that the children I was about to meet were going to be pushovers.

I arrived with Vera the Nera, a toy tin chicken that trundled around in a circle and laid small plastic eggs, and a couple of soft toy hens liberated from thrift stores. One was a slightly anonymous cartoon chicken made in Thirsk by a company called, umm, Furry Friends; the other was a sinister-looking, fuzz-lined giant with big, staring eyes and white pupils. More worryingly, the giant chicken's red wattles, which should have dangled from under its beak, were growing out of its fat chest.

My father, who likes visiting thrift stores, chatting up the old ladies who work in these places and buying cheap clothes and "useful things," saw this chicken mutant and thought I would probably like it. Well, I *quite* like it, but our cat absolutely loves it, enthusiastically rubbing her scent glands into its synthetic fur.

With its huge chest, ungainly wings, and an orange fabric beak that looked as if it had been modeled on a prizefighter's nose, this was a chicken soft toy with the stance of a Tooting nightclub bouncer. A little label near its voluminous ass contained the words DESIGN AND QUALITY. IKEA OF SWEDEN. MADE IN S. KOREA.

A realistic-looking rubber egg completed my ensemble of props. Beyond that I hadn't prepared anything in particular. I wasn't sure what my audience or their caregivers wanted, because, for various logistical reasons, attempts at finding out in advance had drawn a blank.

"What should I talk about?" I asked my wife in a pathetic you-work-in-education kind of way during the bleary, early-morning breakfast before departing for Blackheath.

"Ask them what chickens eat," she said. Since they eat almost anything, this seemed like a good starting point.

Further topics included:

- What do chickens grow on their bodies? (feathers);
- What do chickens make? (eggs); and
- What noises do chickens make? (cue mass cluckings and squawkings).

103

Armed with a vague list of similar call-and-response questions and the suggestion that the attention spans of a group of under-fours would be stretched to the limit after half an hour, I collected Vera and set off for town.

THE CHICKEN MAN COMETH

As a child I went to a nursery school near Kew Green. It was run by a nice old biddy called Miss Gordon, although at the time I thought her name was a single word, "Miscordon," and that she lived at the nursery school, which was actually a large room over a pub billiard hall. We had access to the garden, and I can remember being fascinated by the whirligig clothes dryer at one end of the garden (what did it do?), and getting stuck halfway up a small tree and wailing a lot.

Mostly, my recollections of the place now are more of sensations than specific events, a mix of constant noise, the bright, primary colors, of plastic and wooden toy building blocks, chewing said plastic and wooden blocks, being mesmerized by the swirling tree-ring patterns in the varnished wooden flooring, having my hair pulled, and the strange, yeasty smell of empty wooden beer barrels.

I looked at the Blackheath children doing their stuff, and realized that, even if they'd never so much as snorted a beer barrel, the riotous stimuli that make up the experience of being very young hadn't changed.

As a small aside, I've never tried recreational drugs, partly out of cowardice (and because being stoned seemed to make dull, conformist people duller still), and partly because I've always suspected that, between the ages of zero and four or so, you were gloriously, naturally out of your head anyway, and anything pharmacologically induced would be a poor substitute.

When you're little everything is potentially amazing or unusual, so the appearance of a man with a live chicken was greeted with vague

interest by some of the children, a degree of excitement by others, and total indifference by the rest. Most of them were breezing around a big-lawned garden, chaperoned not by a slightly stern, slightly distant Miscordon, but by girls in their late teens or early twenties, who mostly seemed to be cast from the same plump template.

There was a set of French windows, which led from the nursery itself to a patio area, on which sheets were spread. Soon the children were planted on the sheets, and I was given a garden seat on which to put Vera's travel case. I appropriated one of the old tires that were scattered around the garden as playthings and sat on that.

The children sat in a compact huddle, a small human tide that stopped just before my feet. A small boy with a pensive face gave me a neat, round pebble, and one or two children attempted to wander off, but were intercepted by guarding girls who turned them around and pointed them back the way they had come. There was no escape from the man with the hen.

Vera considered her audience. I started talking, introducing her and trying hard not to think too much about the words I was using. Better a few came out that they didn't understand than that the conversation became a stuttering stop/start mess as I tried to dredge up "appropriate" simple words, or that what I wanted to say was boiled down to meaninglessness as I spent the entire time talking in child pidgin English, a strange language apparently used only by adults.

I asked how many of them had seen a chicken before.

"I have!"

"So have I."

"Well, I saw one too."

"I haven't seen one. I haven't seen one. I haven't seen one."

"It's a chicken."

The voices subsided and I asked where they'd seen one before.

"I have seen one before. It was on an airplane," said a tiny, very serious-looking girl.

A smiling little boy sitting at the front got up, came over to me and peered intently at my forehead.

"I saw one. At the zoo!" he said triumphantly, then stomped off and sat down again.

This resulted in a great chorus of small people telling me that they'd seen chickens in zoos. Later the girl who'd met her chicken on an airplane fell into line and began using the Z word too.

Asking what chickens made produced a gratifying response, with a great many cries of "Eggs! Eggs!"

Producing the fake egg and muttering something about its being very special, I asked if eggs were easy to break. Yes, agreed most of the children, they were.

So I dropped the egg, which bounced in a very satisfactory way. The children were completely underwhelmed, nor did they seem to notice when it struck the side of my head. A further attempt at egg-bouncing was greeted with more incomprehension, so I decided to quit while I was behind and proffered the tin chicken.

Would they like to see it lay some eggs?

"*Yesss!*"

I waggled the "on" switch and was relieved when its innards ground into action. On the patio the fake bird did its revolving, egg-laying stuff and was instantly mobbed, vanishing under a writhing mass of toddlers. This meant that the shyer audience members, who'd sat further back, could just about hear some whirring noises from the toy chicken, but all they could see was a diaper-wearing horde.

Removing a plastic egg from one child who had picked it up and was anxious to see what it tasted like, I did not feel particularly in command. In fact, it had taken about three minutes for me to lose the plot and, before order was restored, a further thirty seconds from the

rather more authoritative caregivers of "Everybody sit down now. *Sit down, please.* Tara, sit there. That's it."

After another small boy had wandered up and offered me a minute, torn piece of scrunched-up paper ("Thank you"), I decided to play my trump card.

"Would you like to see the real chicken?"

This brought an affirmative chorus.

I said something about how chickens flapped their wings, and that some people found this frightening, and, if any of our audience decided they found flapping chicken wings frightening, then it was all right to say so. Then I opened the cat box lid and Vera obligingly hopped out, accompanied by a satisfying chorus of "Oohs."

This seemed like a good time to ask what chickens ate. Cue another cacophony of suggestions.

"Seeds!"

"Apples!"

"Bread!"

"Apples!"

"Eggs!"

"I said *apples*!"

"Bananas!"

We ground to a halt again. This wasn't as easy as it appeared. Then somebody asked Vera's age—a lifeline.

"She's about one year old."

This was quite interesting, but not as interesting as when everybody told me how old they were.

"I'm almost four!" said the boy with the baseball cap. He was soon drowned out by cries of "I'm three!" "Four!" "It's my birthday in September!"

The last observation came from the girl who'd never seen a chicken before (this chicken, by the way, was coping remarkably well

with the volume of information, or just the volume). Seeing a straw to cling to, I asked which day in September the child had her birthday.

She considered for a moment, then said, "September the third."

Bingo! "That's my birthday," I said, grinning idiotically.

You've probably heard the phrase "out of the mouths of babes . . . ," meaning children say completely honest, curdlingly embarrassing things. This child didn't utter a word, but her face spoke volumes—it said, "So?"

I was seized by the inertia of not knowing what to do next, then somebody asked if chickens could fly, so, tickling Vera under the chin, I launched into an overlong, overcomplex explanation about how chickens came from jungles, where they could half run and half fly to get away from animals that wanted to eat them. This was quite an abstract idea, the sort of thing you'd explain to a small bunch of seven-year-olds, rather than a big, rolling mass of preschoolers. Flying and running? Surely it should be one or the other.

You can judge how engaged my audience was when a passing helicopter clattered overhead, its rotor blades noisily slapping the air.

"Helicopter! Helicopter! Helicopter!" they cried, pointing upwards and drowning me out.

Once order was restored I allowed Vera the briefest of walkabouts, since she wasn't interested in the small amount of food scattered on the ground, and seemed moderately happy to join the children. Once she was back in her box, I wondered quite what to do next.

AND THE CHICKEN SAID "TOOK! TOOK! TOOK!"

Salvation came in the form of one of the daycare workers, brandishing two chicken-related storybooks. Yes, I was going to have to read to the children—something I'd never done before. For such a novice, getting the interest of one child would be difficult enough—but twenty-plus?

One book had big pictures, two or three lines of text per page, and a plot that involved a farm, six eggs, and a brown chicken who spent much of the time going "Took! Took! Took! Took! Took!" There were also two white hens, although they weren't called white hens: they were called Leghorns. Leghorn is a chicken breed, something not explained in the text and even more abstract than chickens that can run and fly in the jungle. This was a bit like reading a story about Bill the big brown dog coming home from his walk to be greeted by his friend Maurice, the monocle-wearing Shiatsu.

Actually, the chicken story worked perfectly well. It was a rhythm thing. My audience couldn't care less what a Leghorn actually was. They could latch onto the story, follow where it went and, at strategic moments, join in.

So, I sat on my tire and went "Took! Took! Took!"

"Took! Took! Took! Tooka! Took! Took! Took! Took!" went most of the nursery children, although I did notice one girl with severe black bangs, a tomato-red dress and matching complexion, screwed-up eyes, and a mouth like an unhappy mailbox slit, making determined efforts to escape from an adult's lap.

To help with the narrative flow, I showed the children each picture before going on to the next page.

"I can't see!" said the boy with the cap. If I asked him whether he could see after each page was turned he didn't say a word, but if I failed to do this he would display his excellent diction and projection by telling everyone that he couldn't.

"Took! Took! Took!"

"Took! Took! Took!"

("I can't see!")

"Took! Took! Took!" ad nauseam, until we reached the denouement, where the eggs . . . No, you'll have to read it yourself to find out what happened.

Half an hour had passed, so having once again discussed chickens eating apples, and having answered a query about whether Vera had only one eye (a good point when you're looking closely at an animal with eyes at the sides of its head, if you haven't studied one before), I picked up my various birds, pocketed my rubber egg, and retreated to a back room and a much-needed cup of tea.

GETTING HER CLUCKS IN ORDER

Back home, I decanted a grateful Vera back in the chicken run with the other hens and opened my mail, glad to be back in the ordered, predictable world of adults.

One parcel yielded a CD. "Orriel Smith—*The World's Favorite Cluckoratura Arias*," it said on the cover. With only mild foreboding I put this on the CD player and my house was filled by extracts of Mozart and Offenbach, with the vocal parts clucked rather than sung with demented verve by a lady with a pure opera singer's voice.

Orriel Smith was an American vocalist whose face adorned the CD's cover. She was wearing a sort of masquerade mask made from sequins and chicken feathers. A letter from the lady herself explained that she'd bought *Hen and the Art of Chicken Maintenance*, having seen the book and "squawked with delight." She hoped I would be entertained by the CD, recorded after she decided that a lot of operagoers probably wouldn't notice if their favorite pieces were sung in fluent "chicken."

I pondered the ordered predictability of adults in relation to children, found it wanting, and, with Mozart's "Alleluia" chorus in full squawk, went back into the garden to collect the eggs.

8

Ford Popular?

CAPTIVE AUDIENCE

In a strange way, the next destination for Vera and me had a lot in common with the Lingfield Day Nursery. It was an institution where one group of people had complete control over the lives of another, where routine was fixed and education mixed with containment. It had inmates who would rather have been somewhere else, but had no choice in the matter—how many nursery school attendees go willingly when they first start? Also, they'd been put there for the convenience of others.

Our destination was Ford Open Prison, located in the middle of a sort of English tundra, a few miles inland from where Sussex peters out and subsides into the sea at Littlehampton. This is one of those end-of-the-world places where people seem to wander about in a daze.

We were visiting Ford to talk about books and chickens, as part of an impromptu writers' workshop with added avian interest, and had pulled up on a brutally hot summer's day in August, when hard sunlight mixed unsparingly with oppressive humidity.

These weren't good traveling conditions for hens or humans. We'd arrived early, after a long, fiddly journey that involved a swathe of twisting back roads and crowded, bad-tempered highways. We hadn't even started and I felt sweaty and wrung out. Vera had sat in the far recesses of her travel case drinking regularly and intermittently panting. On arrival I'd decanted some very moist sweet corn into a bowl. Consuming this seemed to have a cooling effect on the bird, who was probably dreaming of a nice dustbath under a tree.

Had I realized just how hot it was going to get, I wouldn't have brought her, but it was too late now, and where we were going next would certainly be cooler than the interior of a parked car. I also had the not very worthy thought that a prison parking lot wouldn't be a good place to leave the windows open.

Arranging a prison visit had involved a good deal of letter-writing and a fair degree of skepticism and mistrust on the part of the authorities. A guy who wants to bring a live chicken to a prison "because I've written a book about hens, and now I'm writing another one" is at best going to be treated with caution.

I'd been told the best way to do this was to approach individual prisons directly, then write to their governors.

Many of the prison telephone receptionists I'd spoken to when first getting in touch with these establishments managed to convey the deep conviction that I was playing a prank while using words and adopting tones that appeared entirely neutral. It had something to do with the pauses.

"A chicken."

(Silence.)

"I see."

(Significant silence.)

"Well then . . . I'll have to put you through to the governor's office."

(Silence pregnant with skepticism and laced with disapproval.)

"Putting you through now." Click.

I would then speak to a secretary or personal assistant, stumbling through my curious request as a second helping of unspoken disbelief trickled out of my phone's earpiece.

On each occasion I was told to write to the governor, e-mail the governor, ditto the prison writer in residence, then call back. Oh, yes, and the chicken might be a problem.

I went through this process with three prisons, but these efforts felt like dropping pebbles into the sea. The letters, e-mails, and phone calls were swallowed up and nothing changed.

Friends were skeptical too. More than one referred to chickens having their necks wrung (and, that unworthy feeling again, the same

thought had occurred to me, but I'd kept it to myself). A prison visitor who saw inmates at Wormwood Scrubs didn't rate my chances of getting anywhere, especially at the higher-security lock-up jails like hers.

So I'd gone for lower-security "open" prisons on the basis that the people who ran them might be more amenable and that there would be less red tape to plow through, but the process still seemed to be sludged up by official inertia.

The signals emanating from Ford seemed no more encouraging than those from the prisons I'd tried before. I'd written, then phoned the governor, only to find she was in a meeting, on vacation, busy.

After three weeks I seemed no further forward. It was a case of "one more try" before starting again somewhere else.

I keyed in the number. She was on site and, yes, I could talk to her. The person on the other end of the phone apologized for the delay. She was friendly and apparently happy that the approach was sincere, thought this could be fun and interesting for the inmates, but warned that it would take a little time to arrange, and I'd have to work with Catherine, Ford's writer in residence, who would be on site in a couple of days.

Catherine turned out to be an expatriate American travel journalist and author who switched from writing travel books and newspaper features to passing on her skills to the diverse range of inmates housed in Ford.

These could range from petty criminals to fine defaulters to boys who'd been in brawls that had degenerated into assaults, drug users who'd turned to crime to pay for their habits, white-collar offenders such as dodgy accountants or people who had been crooked in the City, to Jeffrey Archer, the Mr. Toad of British politics, whose sojourn in Britain's prison system for perjury had taken him to Ford.

He would have shared the canteen, gym, and classrooms with these people, as well as with lifers coming to the end of their sen-

tences and making a staged return to the outside world, and people at the start of their adult lives who were being inexorably sucked into the tougher prisons the lifers were leaving behind.

Acquaintances who knew about these things told me to expect a melting pot of ages, backgrounds, and experiences. As for the staff, they said I was likely to find a degree of professional mistrust, a jaundiced view of human nature, a determination that nobody was going to "put one over on them," an adherence to rules and regulations, and the exercise of often quite small-scale powers that might, under some circumstances, be seen as obstructive, and perhaps be used as part of the process of punishment many regard as the primary function of prison. Stopping things happening was part of their job.

ARMED WITH A CHICKEN

As I say, this was what I'd been told, but I didn't really know what to expect, and as I gathered up Vera in her travel case, and the cat box I used on these trips—which was stuffed with books, photos, the mechanical toy chicken, and a small boom box—I had the strong sensation of getting into a situation for which I was ill prepared.

As I struggled across the parking lot, laden down, and made for the busy road that divided it from the prison entrance, I was greeted by a friendly, senior-looking prison officer, who looked even hotter than we were. "So you've made it, then. A lot of people here didn't think you were really coming. They thought it was a joke."

Later, Catherine told me that this man was a linchpin in overseeing prison security and had been instrumental in agreeing that both Vera and I would be allowed into Ford. If the BBC had twitched about letting a hen into one of its studios, some of the jail staff had gone into a positive spasm at the prospect of allowing one into their jail.

During a flurry of e-mails and phone calls in the weeks before the visit, Catherine had warned me that the idea had made quite a

lot of people pretty restive, and that there was every chance that a live-hen ban would be imposed. I asked about bringing a fake one as a fallback, which she seemed to think would suffice.

One guard who apparently kept chickens wanted to know if Vera had been inoculated, then expressed fears the bird might give one of the prisoners a horrible disease. Another objection was that Ford's sniffer dogs would be "put off" by her scent. In what way wasn't made clear.

Having been drip-fed all this bad news in advance, I was surprised and delighted when it was decided that both of us would be welcome after all, but I was given very specific instructions about when and how Vera and I were to arrive and what I was to do. One of those instructions was that she should stay in the car when I first checked in, just in case there was a last-minute change of heart.

The subtropical temperatures coupled with the likelihood that I would end up with an instantly basted, fully feathered chicken if Vera didn't come with me, meant that I forgot and arrived at the stark reception area both earlier than expected and not as instructed.

I asked a middle-aged woman behind a glass screen if she'd mind letting Catherine know we'd arrived. Commenting that she'd heard about the visit, but also thought it was a joke, she picked up a phone and made a call.

When Catherine appeared she saw the chicken and a look of concern crossed her face.

"He hasn't arrived at the right time, and he brought the chicken with him," said the lady behind the glass. She spoke without rancor or emphasis, but, sensing it could spell trouble, I apologized, explained about the heat and the potential for the bird to be cooked if left in the car, then offered to go back and wait with her, but was told to stay put while further phone calls were made.

"They'll need to be searched, and we'll have to find someone to do that," added the glass-partition woman. Vera and I were due to be interviewed by one of Catherine's protégés, but rules were rules.

You could understand it. I was a journalist with a chicken, and potentially, an ulterior motive. Smuggling a weapon or some sort of contraband along with the bird would have provided all the raw material for a shock horror tabloid spread (WHAT A CLUCKUP! Egg on face as prison birdbrains let armed and dangerous chicken man into Archer jail, etc.).

THE FRISKING OF VERA

Not making a fuss seemed the best policy, and the potential crisis apparently passed when, ten minutes later, an amused, easygoing prison

officer ushered me into a back room for searching purposes. Everything was checked in a relaxed but thorough way. We left Vera till last.

"Have you ever searched a chicken before?" I asked.

"No," said the guard, who decided a noninvasive approach would be best. It was clear that she hadn't been pre-stuffed. I held the slightly protesting bird at various angles until the man was satisfied that there was nothing untoward.

"That's fine," he said as I decanted a grateful chicken back into her box, and rejoined Catherine. We were ushered through another door and into the main prison complex.

Ford is built on the site of an old air base. It still has that slightly grim military look to it, with what was presumably once a parade ground at its center surrounded by a mixture of aging barracks-like structures, and, later, blockish brick buildings.

"We'll go to my office," said Catherine, a quietly determined, middle-aged woman with a shock of ginger hair. We were approached by a stocky, forty-something black man with a bull neck, shaven head, and shy, diffident manner. A prisoner, the first I'd met.

"Ray!" said Catherine, who sounded relieved. This was her interviewer. He'd been out on work duty, and been held up trying to be let into the prison to meet us. Later, I was to be told half-jokingly by a number of inmates that it was easier to get out of Ford than to get back in again.

We exchanged a few pleasantries ("So this is your chicken, then? Ha, ha!"). Ray insisted on carrying the cat box laden with stuff for the talk, and we trudged next to a long ugly building with a big cafeteria, and past a water garden. I noticed the parade ground area was alive with rabbits, which seemed very tame, and when I commented on this somebody made a remark about overpopulation and imminent gassing.

Everywhere we looked there were men in identical clothes who appeared to be hanging around waiting for something to happen. I mentioned this to Catherine and she said the inmates were more or less standing by their beds before being allowed to move on to amenities such as the gym. Soon there would be a rush to whatever activities were available. It was a case of first come, first served.

We made our way into a nondescript building and up a flight of ugly concrete stairs to a gloomy, echoing landing. Catherine unlocked a door that led into her office, and Ray, Vera, and I trooped in after her and gratefully collapsed into the well-used chairs that dotted its interior.

As I refilled Vera's water bowl and sorted out some more food for the bird, we carried on a rather stilted conversation. What was off limits? ("So, what are you inside for?") Could an innocent remark cause offense? He seemed a very self-effacing man.

We looked at some of the pieces he'd written for the *Fordster* magazine (a name surely coined by someone with a sense of humor), and I sensed a perceptible ratcheting up of the man's shyness. What I was reading meant more to its author than just words on a page.

He asked if I would mind terribly if we got on with the interview as he'd been working all day in the nightmare heat, was bathed in sweat, and would like to shower, change, and eat something before coming to the chicken talk.

He'd prepared a list of questions and, as I began to twitter back approximations of answers, he began the laborious process of writing down the answers. As someone who never learned shorthand, and has lousy handwriting, I could sympathize. Ray mentioned a Dictaphone and made the slightly wistful remark about the lack of cassette tapes.

"Hang on a minute," I said, reaching for the boom box brought along to entertain the prisoners with a quick blast of *The World's*

Favorite Cluckoratura Arias. I pressed the cassette eject button and the drawer slid open to reveal a C90 tape.

My wife, an otherwise sane, sensible person, listens to *The Archers* on Radio 4, and when she risks missing an episode (or "dose," to give it its proper medical name) of this soap opera of British rural life, she gets me to record it. Although I live in the country, I detest this everyday story of country folk. Am I alone in thinking they're country folk you'd move to an urban ghetto to avoid?

Confessing this is likely to result in hate mail. If you love them, don't let me put you off, but I know someone who says the theme tune always makes him think of self-abuse.

So my cassette was filled with the bleating, whining, terrible fake yokel vocal moaning, weeping, emotional "breathing out" noises, "I'm a bad ass" growling, and rib-tickling, mannered, social-climber voices that have been keeping *Archers* addicts happy for the past 8,000 years.

I gladly proffered the tape to Ray. "Would you like to record the interview with this?"

Freed from the constraint of looking at his ballpoint squiggling up and down at a normal writing speed, I chattered about things chicken-related. "What made you choose Ford?" said Ray. Should I dissemble? The primary reason was that Archer had been there, so I'd heard of the place and was interested to see it, but in the company of this man this now seemed cheap and nasty. I'd also labored under the delusion that it wasn't very far from where I lived, and it was also the only prison to agree to our visit, so I dwelled on these reasons.

At the end of the interview Ray asked his killer question. "Why did the chicken cross the road?" Answers on a postcard, please.

Since there was a two-hour gap before Vera and I met up with Ray's cohabitees, Catherine suggested finding something to eat, so, leaving Vera locked up in her cool, well-ventilated office, we went through the logistical hoops of legitimately exiting a prison and

drove to Littlehampton, which squatted under the unrelenting sun, sweating along with pink-fleshed families who seemed to make up its itinerant, vacationing population. They sat on walls scowling at the harsh, white light or each other, while sun-burnt children were chastised and tattoos sizzled.

Fish and chips wouldn't have been my first choice for a late-afternoon meal in a heat wave, but the list of alternatives was limited. Catherine and I joined a slowly melting line in a place where you waited while they cooked your fish, frying along with it as the minutes ticked by.

We talked about the iniquities of being a freelance journalist, trying to teach writing techniques to men who in some cases might still be acquiring basic literacy skills, how alleged, illicit visits by prisoners to the nearest supermarket had made the local paper. All the while perspiring people in kitchen whites spent forever preparing our food.

When it came we were at least half an hour older than when we'd ordered. The car was a good ten minutes' walk away and time was starting to run out.

So that was why we ended up on a bench in a parched, formal-looking garden across the road from the prison. This was maintained by the prisoners, and was once a meeting place for their families, which at least offered a little privacy, but, thanks to its being used also as a rendezvous for drug deals, these get-togethers had been banned.

There was no shade, so we ate and leaked like human shower-heads until it was time to collect Vera and do our stuff.

We made our weary way around the parade ground, attracting comments from staff and inmates alike, which seemed to indicate that most of them thought the posters Catherine had put up about our visit were jokes, too.

About fourteen prisoners came to see us in a sultry classroom with desks and chairs more or less made into a square around its

walls. Vera and I ended up in the center of this. A couple of the inmates sat behind us, which was slightly disconcerting.

Every so often I'd turn Vera's box, or crane my neck to speak directly to them.

MEET MY CHICKEN

Our audience ranged from a soft-spoken man in his seventies to a tall, rangy, distracted-looking youth. The others who stick in my mind included Ray and two bearded fifty-somethings. One was intense and wiry, the other chunkier and less careworn. For a brief, unpleasant moment I thought I'd once worked with this man. How do you make light conversation with someone you haven't seen for fifteen years whom you happen to meet in prison? "Lovely to see you here. Would you like to meet my chicken?" Discovering that this was the first time we'd met was a relief.

There was also a powerfully built man in his thirties with still, appraising eyes and an angular, unsmiling face framed by a trace of beard. He half-sat, half-slouched in the corner of the room and did absolutely nothing, but the longer I talked the more I became aware of his presence and the more disconcerted I felt by it. He seemed to be the product of a world I knew nothing about. Chickens surely weren't his thing.

I did the usual conversational icebreakers. Had anybody kept hens, or grown up with them?

There were nods from some of the older men, and the guy I'd thought I knew said he'd bred a variety of birds.

How about writing? Catherine was anxious for me to talk about the process of getting into print, the work, and necessary compromises involved. She'd said that some of the men who attended her class—particularly the white-collar brigade—wanted to write huge tracts about the unfairness of the prison regulations. Often these

things tended to be mixtures of denial and self-justification, which, given that their authors were locked up for having broken the law, rather limited their appeal. She said some of her students found this hard to grasp.

"I write," said the tall, fidgeting youth. Prompted by Catherine, I tried to find out what he wrote, but what he said in reply seemed circular and unclear, although the answer ultimately appeared to be "what I want to."

Deciding it wasn't yet time to introduce Vera, I kept talking, although I did not feel that it was going terribly well. The conversational ebb and flow that had served in bookshops was only partially connecting here. Like a flickering lamp with a loose wire, what I said about Vera's background, my background, book writing, sex-change chickens, and so forth engaged only some of the inmates some of the time. I was quickly running out of options, and had even left the *Cluckoratura Arias* CD in Catherine's office, although, as with the tin chicken, I somehow felt this audience would not have greeted this entertainment warmly.

The slouching man was managing to convey dissatisfaction with a combination of immobility and the hard, level stare. It was disquieting (in retrospect, I don't think that was the intention), as he gave off disappointed and pissed-off signals. Eventually he spoke.

"I know more about this than he does."

"Did you breed chickens?" I asked.

"I used to breed Black Rocks." My preconception of him had been absolutely wrong. He wasn't unhappy because chickens *weren't* his thing: he was unhappy because they *were*. Further probing yielded some terse answers that quickly established him as a man who knew.

"Well, I'm an amateur. We just keep a few birds for fun. I'm sure you know more about the differences of breeds and rearing birds than I do."

123

Yes, he said evenly, that was obvious. He'd come to learn something new, and it didn't look as if there was much for him here.

Perhaps, I thought, we could persuade him to share what he knew, bring his expertise into the conversation, dragging something positive from a sticky situation.

Some of the other inmates had been happy to talk about themselves, their lives and interests. This man wasn't. He had nothing to prove and hadn't come to contribute. Why should he?

The atmosphere did lighten a bit, but after another five minutes he decided enough was enough, stood up, said he was going to the gym. "I'm not getting anything out of this," he said. "No disrespect to you."

Then he was gone. Soon afterwards the tall boy who'd said he was a writer headed for the exit and eventually Ray got up, shook my hand warmly, and said he, too, had other commitments.

"Nice meeting you—and your chicken."

THE CHICKEN WHISPERER

If this rate of attrition kept up, Vera and I would end up trying to entertain Catherine and nobody else.

"Can I look at the bird?"

It was the guy with the beard who'd kept chickens.

Here goes, I thought, as the unworthy part of my mind dredged up the comments about neck-wringing. As I handed Vera over, I felt bad for thinking like this, but . . .

The man handled Vera carefully and started talking about her shape, plumage, and general health, which he pronounced as good. Then it happened.

"I can make a chicken go to sleep," he said. In an instant he had clasped Vera's head and was twisting her neck downwards. The sense of dread I felt lasted for less than a second. The man carefully guided Vera's head under one of her wings and gently pressed this against his chest.

"She'll sleep now," he said.

I felt like a complete heel. Vera felt wide awake. Her head instantly popped out from under her wing. She blinked and looked mildly affronted. The Bird Man of HMP Ford had two or three more goes at persuading her that a quiet nap was just what she needed. Vera wouldn't cooperate, but I could see that, given enough time, and perhaps more familiar surroundings, his technique would have had the desired result.

As the man handed back an unruffled but determinedly unsleeping chicken, the formal-talk element of what we were trying to do painlessly fell to pieces, despite a couple of attempts by Catherine to drag it to something vaguely "educational."

I'd prattle on for a bit, which would spark a thought or an idea, and the inmates would begin talking among themselves, discussing aspects of their lives, from the Triumph Spitfire once owned by the elderly prisoner's daughter, a slightly melancholic-looking man, to a fellow inmate suddenly being transferred from Ford to another prison, not being allowed to take his books, spending hours hanging around with nothing to do, then being sent back. There were commiserations and stories of similar experiences, and I began to get a smallest glimpse of the powerlessness of prison life, of being either passively or actively under the thumb, even in a place like Ford, where prisoners had keys to their cells and where media for training and rehabilitation seemed to be a serious part of the regime.

In the process, Vera and I had gone from being the center of attention to observers and occasional participants. What these people really wanted to do was talk about themselves and their various shared experiences.

For some reason the conversation came around to the antiques shop owned by Ronnie Barker, the comedian and actor. The older inmate mentioned that he'd been there once.

"I've written for Ronnie Barker," said the chicken whisperer, who said he'd been a professional scriptwriter and had plans for a novel. I'd been told to expect a social melting pot in a prison, and that was what I'd found. What he and his fellow inmates had gotten from meeting Vera and me was less tangible. I'd been billed as some sort of expert on domestic birds and writing, and had gone to a prison where I'd met people who probably had nothing to learn from me on either subject.

I ached to ask why the script/chicken man had ended up at Ford, but something stopped me.

THE TELLER OF TALES

"It's not done to ask people why they're inside," said Catherine an hour or so later. We were sitting in the garden of a forbidding-looking pub a couple of miles from the prison. So I didn't find out why the scriptwriter was at Ford, although I subsequently discovered that two of the other audience members were lifers. Which ones? Well, that's their secret.

"You'd have had a bigger audience at one of the higher-category prisons, where people are in lock-up twenty-three hours a day sometimes," said Catherine. A captive audience in every sense, unlike the men who'd come to see us. Were Vera and I part of the process of re-habilitation? I wasn't sure.

The pub was next to a run-down railway station and, although both appeared to be in the middle of nowhere, a steady procession of dusty-looking electric trains whined in and out. It was getting dark as prerecorded announcements about where they were going boomed out over the hot, ugly countryside. The trains offered a means of escape to the outside world, away from the closed community of the prison with its rules, codes, and a simmering sense of . . .

what? Impotence? Anger? Frustration? All those things probably, but more specifically, sadness, or being sad in a generic rather than pathetic way.

"Have you been to a prison before?" asked Catherine, when I talked to her about how the place felt to me. When I told her no, she spoke about the regime and the inmates and staff in a way that indicated that she thought I'd missed the point.

She mentioned a prisoner coming to the end of a two-year stretch who talked to her about his first supervised visit to Littlehampton and his sense "of being normal" as he browsed in a record shop, where he was chatted up by a couple of girls, and then bought an ice cream—and had the cash to do this.

Then there was the man to whom she had taught basic literacy skills, who then revealed himself to be a "brilliant" story writer, and began writing stuff for his daughter. Catherine also talked about how both newly arrived staff and prisoners, who were used to more prescriptive jails, found the way Ford worked to be disconcerting and alarming. Making decisions and confronting choices is tough when you've grown used to having other people make them for you.

Later, back in the car, Vera slept and I drove with the windows down and cool air rushing in, aware that this tin box on wheels represented personal space and privacy. Turning up the radio, I wondered how long it would take to get home to my own bed.

9

Hen on the Hill

THE STAR & GARTER

On days out to Richmond Park near London, we used to see Charlie Hankins. He was a compact, forceful-looking man sitting in a curious hand-propelled wheelchair. Dating from World War II, this had two levers to make it go, and he would be rowing along one of the pathways that radiate into the park's interior.

We knew he was a resident of the Royal Star & Garter Home, an imperious, Edwardian structure perched on the top of Richmond Hill. To us he was a human landmark, but at the time we didn't know his name or how he came to be there.

Years later I drove through the park to the Star & Garter with Vera, to meet some of the other people who lived there. I also hoped to find out more about the man in the wheelchair, who, in part, was the inspiration for our visit.

The Star & Garter building is a landmark for people who live in the area, and home to ex-service personnel, both men and women. It dates from 1924, but looks older, and is the product of those sorts of grand public gestures that have since fallen out of fashion.

During World War I, Queen Mary—wife of George V and grandmother of Queen Elizabeth II—called for a permanent, specialist facility to be built for some of the thousands of service personnel who'd been wounded. With funds raised by the Auctioneers and Estate Agents' Institute (there's a joke here about real estate agents not being true to type, but we'll let that one pass), the run-down Star & Garter Hotel on Richmond Hill was bought for the purpose. The place had fallen on hard times since the days when guests had included Charles Dickens and Alfred, Lord Tennyson, and in 1916 its ballroom and banqueting hall were filled with the first sixty-five wounded men.

A huge ballroom is hardly an ideal place in which to convalesce, especially if you're bedridden, and eight years later the old hotel made way for the current home, paid for by public subscription—for the equivalent of almost $16.5 million—raised by the British Women's Hospital Committee.

The place has a very simple credo: Anyone with a military background who has been disabled, even in civilian life, is potentially entitled to the care it offers, ranging from full residential to respite and day care, a variety of therapies, and things to do, such as going to see a guy with a hen. I'd wanted to take a chicken to an old people's home and meet the residents. The Star & Garter idea grew from this.

When first opened, the home was largely populated by young men. Pictures of the 1924 opening show King George and Queen Mary greeting people in their twenties and thirties, but, although it remains open to present-day service personnel, the people who live there permanently are increasingly elderly.

"The average age of our residents is eighty-five," said Sue Viney, the home's activities and welfare coordinator. We were walking into the home's big, stone-clad atrium. Sue had met us in the parking lot and insisted on carrying Vera's travel case. It turned out that she was a chicken fan.

Soon I'd found out about Charlie Hankins, who had arrived at the Star & Garter in 1970 and died just a few months before our visit. In 1943, Hankins had been a twenty-two-year-old soldier in the Black Watch, Royal Highland Regiment, in North Africa. Near Tunis he was hit by mortar fire, suffered chest wounds, and lost both legs and the sight in one eye. This didn't stop him swimming, skydiving, and scuba diving in Loch Ness to raise funds for the home. And that spindly chair took him from John O'Groats to Land's End in 1986. Six years later he did the trip in reverse. In the end he raised more than $550,000 for the home.

The human landmark had become a remarkable man, and the more I found out about Charlie Hankins, the more I regretted not having met him, but Vera and I were about to spend time with some of his contemporaries. I just hoped that we would provide a mildly entertaining diversion.

I'd never been inside the Star & Garter building, but had driven past it hundreds of times. Although very much an old-fashioned In-stitution—with a capital "I"—it lacked the end-of-the-line misery that seems to sweat from the walls of some nursing homes. Its opu-lence and scale all seemed to be a big architectural thank-you for the people it was built to serve, although the place seemed oddly empty.

We made our way through an impressive area, which Sue said was called the Queen's Room. It overlooked a simple, semi-enclosed terraced garden with a fountain in its center. At the end of that was the famous view from Richmond Hill overlooking the River Thames where it cranks to the right and slides away toward Twickenham.

"We thought about getting you both to talk in here, but some people might have difficulty hearing," said Sue as we made our way from this echoing space that could accommodate a small orchestra and audience, and headed for a smaller, more intimate room that also opened onto the terrace.

A man in a wheelchair slept peacefully as the other people who'd come to see us arrived. Most were also wheelchair-bound and elderly. They milled about and arranged themselves into a semicircle and waited for things to get going.

Since our trip to Ford Prison I'd carried out a bit of a postmortem on the elements that worked there, and the things that didn't. I'd made the mistake of trying to talk at, and almost through, the people at Ford in an ultimately pointless attempt to direct what was said.

This time I'd try to use Vera's presence as a conversational springboard, talking about the bird and her life, ancestry, and so on, to fill in the gaps when the people who'd come to see her had nothing to say.

WHY THE CHICKENS CROSSED THE ROAD

This proved to be a good move. Peggy Starkie, who'd been in the British Women's Royal Naval Service during World War II, talked enthusiastically about the arrival of some hens at her home—in Sloane Square. Between 1939 and 1945, a lot of city dwellers bought chickens as a way of feeding themselves.

When the birds acquired by Peggy Starkie's family arrived, the henhouse that was being built for them wasn't entirely finished, so the flock escaped, improving their road sense by rushing about Sloane Square and doing their best to evade capture.

"Do you know anything about turkeys?" asked a smiling old gent. I confessed that I didn't.

"I was attacked by a turkey. Vicious thing. I had a broom and it came up the broom and went for me with its claws." At the recollection of

being assaulted by a psychopathic uncooked Christmas dinner, this man managed to look even happier than at the beginning of his recollection.

As we talked, people would roll up to the door, look in, move on, or decide that this was sufficiently interesting to join the group, resulting in a gentle pause as further rearranging took place.

"Can I just say thank you." It was the turkey man again. "The last time you came with all those little birds. I really enjoyed that."

Some of the residents and a couple of the staff pointed out that this was our first visit. I said something about being happy to take the

credit even if someone else had done all the work. The gent continued to smile broadly.

Now seemed like a good time to introduce Vera. Warning that she wasn't housetrained, I opened the lid of the travel case and the bird hopped out.

This woke a number of residents who had nodded off ("Something like this washes over them in a pleasant way," said Sue).

Sue had once kept chickens and said something about hypnotizing them. She came over and I wondered whether we were about to experience a repeat of the head-under-the-wing incident; but, no, she placed one of her fingers at the top of Vera's beak and began gently stroking toward the tip. The bird grew still and I could feel her relax.

It's apparently possible to draw lines on the ground and, using this hypnotic beak massage, get a bird to lower its head until its beak is on the floor and its owner is mesmerized and staring, presumably in a cross-eyed way, at the line.

Vera's jungle- and tree-dwelling origins were mentioned, and I said that if the bird was hiding on a windblown tree branch her head would stay still as the rest of her rode up and down with the tree. It was a way of seeing things that might want to eat you before they saw you. Picking up Vera, I gently cycled her body from side to side then up and down, while her head stayed still and steady as a spirit level on a Victorian fireplace.

There have been occasions when I've tried this with other birds and they've decided not to play along and become as rigid as something in a freezer, but, since Vera had been happy to cooperate, I asked if everybody else would like to meet her.

Yes, that would be nice. The bird and I gently processed around the room. Hands reached out and caressed feathers while fingers tickled under Vera's chin. Chickens aren't noted for being tactile, but Vera was giving the lie to this.

135

"Isn't she warm?"

"Hello, dear. You are pretty."

"She feels lovely. So soft."

"She's shaking," said an elderly lady.

It was true. The bird didn't struggle or flinch, but this wasn't her idea of fun and she was no longer physically relaxed. I could feel that her sinews had tightened, causing the slight, perceptible tremor that the resident had picked up.

Everyone had been very gentle, but being offered up in this way was clearly causing the bird stress. She just found it frightening.

Only a few people in the room hadn't seen Vera at close quarters. I was left with a dilemma. Should I remove her from the cause of her stress or disappoint the few people who had yet to see her? I chose the path of least resistance and we pressed on. Vera was soon back in her travel case and busying herself with some raisins. Like many animals, hens seem to live entirely in the present; removed from something she wasn't keen on and presented with something she liked, Vera just got on with enjoying it.

MOONLIGHT EGGS

It didn't seem long before Sue was saying in a kind but firm way that everyone had enjoyed meeting Vera and me, and thanking us for visiting. During a low-speed stampede for the exit I found myself shaking hands and thanking the hands' owners for coming to see us.

"I grew up in Norfolk," said a white-haired gent as the last of the wheelchairs filed past. "They put electric lights in the chicken coops to make the birds lay more eggs. Some of the locals wouldn't eat those eggs. They'd say, 'I'm not touching no moonlight eggs.' That's people from Norfolk for you."

"That was Ted Bonnett," said Sue Viney when I told her the story. "He was in the Coldstream Guards during World War II. One

136

Sunday he was walking with his wife in London, but normally he would have been in church with his regiment. Ted was lucky, as the church was hit by a bomb and a lot of his comrades were killed. He could have been there too."

I'd been offered some tea, but en route to Sue's office Vera and I were hailed by a tall, frail lady.

"Is that the chicken? I'd so wanted to come and see it, but I couldn't get in." Time for a brief, avian encore. Vera's stage fright seemed to have deserted her, so I plonked the travel case next to her new admirer and opened the lid. Vera did her hopping-out-and-perching routine, much to the lady's delight, and the three of us spent the next five minutes or so happily ensconced.

Afterwards, Sue showed me around, and the reason for the apparent lack of residents, and their age profile, became clear. "We're leaving. I can hardly bear to think about it, although I can see why we have to," she said as we walked onto the terrace.

Although it was still younger than many of the people living in it, age has been catching up with the grand old Star & Garter building. Sue said that about half the money spent on the place went toward keeping it heated, and trying to convert open wards that were entirely acceptable in 1924 into the single rooms required now had proved thoroughly awkward.

The fact that as a piece of real estate the place was worth a staggering amount of money couldn't be ignored, either. The proceeds of selling it would pretty well pay for three new Star & Garter homes, which apparently is the idea.

They'll have modern facilities, and presumably will be on a more human scale, but they won't have the feeling of history and continuity, the sense of being part of a special community, nor that fabulous view. The people Vera and I met on Richmond Hill were at home here, in the sense that this was their home, and we were their guests.

137

IT'S A BUGGER

I once had the misfortune to meet an idiotic hospital personnel director with a self-conscious beard and a bow tie, who dared describe hospital wards as "the shop floor" and patients as "the product." This was a crassly diminishing way to look at human beings, and a million miles from the atmosphere of this apparently formal, starchy building with its old-fashioned light fittings, spiral stone staircases, and marbled hallways and atrium.

As Vera and I were leaving, Sue Viney asked if I'd noticed that something was missing. "There isn't a smell of pee," she said simply. "We don't have carpets in this part of the building. With carpets, once there's been an accident you can never quite get rid of it." The things that allow us to hang onto our dignity are sometimes surprising.

The actress Dame Peggy Ashcroft is said to have described old age as "a bugger." At the start of our chicken-traveling activities I'd seen enough of its buggerish side to know this is sometimes, but not always, true. The people we'd met here weren't immune from its privations, but they put this into some sort of perspective.

I was given a commemorative book called *I Vow To Thee My Country*, filled with pictures, illustrations, and photographs relating to the home and everything from the *Mary Rose* to the first Gulf War. On page twenty-seven there was a photograph of some World War I airmen, "from No. 22 Squadron," taken on the day in 1918 when the RAF was created by merging the Royal Flying Corps and the Royal Naval Air Service. One of them is John Gurdon, my grandfather.

"We hope you'll come back," said Sue Viney. I plan to.

10

Birdbrains

ON THE TILES

"Look closely at the tiles. What can you see?" asked the man in the pub urinal.

The pair of us were making use of the facilities of the unfeasibly scenic Crown Inn, a pub in the appropriately named Oxfordshire village of Pishil. This wasn't a George Michael moment, nor was it a drunken challenge to fisticuffs ("Look closely at the fuckin' tiles—wha' can yer see, pal?"), so I squinted and saw random brown squiggly lines on lumpy white tiles. It made me think of 1977 rather than anything in particular.

"We used to have tiles like that in our kitchen," said the pub urinal man. He spoke with an accent that I couldn't quite place. "If you look closely you can see the shape of a chicken in each one."

I looked again, and, yes, quite distinct hen outlines had started to make themselves apparent. These were slightly deformed chickens, and they seemed to be running up very steep hills, but they could be nothing else.

At this point I might pretend that I saw them as representing a small epiphany on the road I was traveling with my chicken—after all, these were hens in a place you wouldn't expect to find them—but no: I just registered sort-of chickens on the wall of a pub toilet.

The man's accent was intriguing, and, having tucked myself in, I asked where he came from, since he sounded vaguely Northern, but the cadences of his speech had been blunted, presumably by exposure to the soft south.

"Durham originally," he said.

By way of conversation I mentioned that my wife had gone to university there.

"Oh, right," he said as we trundled back to the bar. "I was more 'town' than 'gown.' In fact, we used to beat up 'gown' on a Friday night."

Having finished this badinage we parted company and I went back to Jane, who was never beaten up by anybody in Durham, perhaps because she looked like somebody who was training to be a teacher—which she was—rather than a prototype merchant banker. Durham in gown guise seems to have produced quite a few people from this template ("the heartless heart/the chinless chin," to quote a Kirsty MacColl lyric).

THE HI-TECH HENHOUSE

Jane, Vera, and I were en route to a village called Wardington, near Banbury, home of the Eglu: a tiny, expensive, plastic henhouse with a chicken run attached to it. This was the product of four former Royal College of Art (RCA) students who'd got the thing into production and created a bit of a stir in the process. Meeting them and bringing one of our chickens to road-test an Eglu fitted in with the ethos of this book.

Jane had expressed a wish to explore Banbury's retail-therapy possibilities, so we dropped her off in the town and set off to the farm/light industrial complex where James Tuthill, William Windham, Johannes Paul, and Simon Nicholls—the Eglu Four—had encamped.

This was hidden at the end of a lane, around the corner from where James Tuthill's uncle made a living tinkering with old Porsches.

Clasping Vera's box, I met William Windham. Bespectacled, tall, and narrow, he was topped off with a mass of wavy hair and an unashamedly large, 1970s Open University lecturer's beard, behind which was the face of someone who looked about twelve, but was presumably in his early twenties, lucky sod.

Divested of Vera's cat box, we decamped to a higgledy-piggledy-looking office building, where bags of chicken feed were leaning against walls covered with mysterious-looking technical drawings,

141

and where oddly shaped plastic pieces shared space with model comedy hens, opened boxes of cookies, teacups, and the detritus of a room where people think as well as work.

William was happy to ascribe the original hi-tech henhouse idea to James Tuthill.

"James kept chickens at the university and built them a little pad, then brought them home. His mother reckoned they needed a bigger and better home."

The quartet had all started life in various bits of countryside ("We all grew up in the middle of nowhere"), and were used to being around animals. William mentioned that the mother of one had a small farm. "Only it's getting larger all the time. I think she's got rather a lot of bantams at the moment. The bloody things are all going broody."

At the RCA, James had to come up with a design project and "decided a henhouse was the way to go," and when he, Windham, and their putative designer friends realized they wanted to work together and looked at their various ideas for things such as lighting, it was decided that a small, expensive henhouse made of plastic was the most commercially viable product.

"There was," said William, "quite a lot of skepticism. You had to pinch yourself sometimes and think, What am I doing?"

What they did was build a series of prototypes and, thanks to a small article in the *Banbury Guardian*, persuaded people who lived nearby to try them out. The design idea was that there should be enough room for a couple of birds in the henhouse, and that they should have access to a reasonably foxproof run area.

"The prototypes weren't exactly pretty, but testing them like this meant we could work out layouts and size to make them really manageable for two chickens," said William. "We changed the design a bit, with really simple things like where to put the nesting box. You'd

think it would be best at the darkest place in the back." (It ended up at the side: apparently, this made collecting the eggs less of a drag.) At one point the idea was that the henhouse could double as a seat, allowing owners to sit and look dotingly at their birds.

Different types of doors were tried before it was decided to go for one that looked rather like a big, hinged paddle, with a simple, round, plunger-like handle at the top to open, close, and lock it.

One prototype featured a door with a guillotine action, which a child of one of the testers took great pleasure in bringing down on the necks of the unfortunate chickens every time they tried venturing out, so that was changed.

"We now take the door mechanism for granted, but at one point we were looking at lengths of string and assorted bits and pieces, before we ended up with a nice, simple solution."

I had been told that James was on the premises but in bed, having been on delivery driving duties the previous day and having staggered

back from Brighton in the small hours. Eventually he appeared: slight, curly-headed, and looking only moderately bleary-eyed.

We discussed double-skinned plastic structures (their henhouse has a sort of air gap between the inner and outer walls to keep the inside cool in summer and insulated in winter), and how they'd found a plastic molding process called rotor molding, which didn't cost a lot to use. Apparently, injection-molding parts, even for something tiny such as a retractable pen top, is hideously expensive.

At this point William dug out a sectioned Eglu to show where the various bits and pieces went. There was something vaguely unsettling about this. "It looks slightly medical," he said cheerfully, putting into words the thought I'd been groping toward. Red, rounded, and comprising a series of strange shapes and recesses, it reminded me strongly of one of those school biology room models of a head, the ones with lurid half-tongues and half-eyeballs. Even the Eglu's plan drawings had a skeletal quality, looking more than a little like a bird's skull.

LOONY 'TOONS

The conversation turned to chicken-related websites. "They say things like 'Eat your chicken if it's ill, or if it dies'—that can't be right," said William.

James mentioned delivering an Eglu to a precocious nine-year-old boy in Dulwich, who said very firmly when he arrived, "You have to come upstairs and look at my cartoons," which were, naturally, chicken-related.

"He's got his own website now," said James, and it wasn't long before I was being shown the results of Junior's labors, which involved a determined yellow animated chicken scudding about over a suitably abstract cartoon Eglu, then finding itself, if not behind bars, then at least behind wire mesh, which caused William to say something about "game over."

The way the hen did what it did brought to mind a children's television program called *Crystal Tips and Alistair*, although the website's drawings and movements were rather better.

In *Crystal Tips and Alistair*, an animated girl-and-dog combo used to jerk around crudely on children's television before the news came on. Crystal Tips, the human element of the partnership, had enormous, strangely triangulated red hair, and was wittily known to millions of schoolboys as "Crystal Tits." Alistair was a large mastiff whose legs appeared to have been broken, given the way they flailed about when he moved.

This had a lot to do with the fact that the drawings were two-dimensional cutouts, and the show's use of precomputer, stop-frame animation, in which the limbs were moved fractionally again and again, and photographed with each little jerk.

William and James were now on something of a roll with chicken websites. "What about that lady in Newcastle? She's got one." A few keystrokes later and we were looking at photos of a 'toon chicken doing chicken-style things. These were accompanied by captions that said things like, "Sybil scratching around in the bamboo." Sybil was clearly a very loved hen, but one whose every poo and peck could be recorded for the entertainment of others.

William and James reckoned they and their partners were dyslexic—something allegedly true of many designers, which may help explain why they seem to think so effectively in visual terms. James said apostrophes baffled him and that mistakes had crept onto their website, resulting in a number of stern "look what you've done" e-mails putting them right. He wrote back to one especially fierce lady thanking her and asking whether, if she saw any other mistakes, she would please point them out. Future dispatches became rather motherly.

The door was open and a small white hen slipped into the room and started pottering about, perhaps with the intention of making a

raid on any cookie crumbs on the floor or the bags of feed standing in a corner. William poked about under one of the tables and extracted a similarly albino egg. The bird was a regular visitor and the two had once been intimately acquainted.

She was slim, pretty as chickens go, but not exactly friendly. "We'd like to sell birds like that, but they're too flighty, too nervous," said William as the white hen made for the exit. The Eglu Four had decided to sell chickens as part of a starter package of henhouse, run, and chicken accessories such as egg cartons, the idea being to attract virgin, and very probably urban, chicken keepers. It had gotten them a lot of column inches in the newspapers, and a lot of interest.

We were now reaching an "Er, what next?" point, so it was decided to have a tour of the facilities, a series of outbuildings that were destined to contain either chickens to go with the henhouses, or bits of henhouse and timber for their slatted wooden floor areas, which was being cut and made up by Simon Nicholls. He and the other three take turns dealing with inquiries and paperwork, assembling the henhouses, and delivering them, which explained the absence of Johannes Paul, who was somewhere north of Watford in a Mercedes Sprinter van.

The only Eglu to be seen assembled and in use contained a rabbit rather than a chicken. Nearly all the birds I saw were running around enjoying the fruits of the farmhouse garden and the surrounding area. They weren't penned up, but this was, after all, a farm.

As we looked at the Eglu-bound rabbit, William remembered another unlikely-sounding part of their research-and-development program. "We put a webcam inside one of the prototypes to see what the chickens did," he said. "It got quite fascinating. We found that we kept watching this chicken movie."

VERA TAKES WING

Back in the design office Vera was procured and released for photographic purposes. James plonked the bird on his lap, tickled her breastplate, then added, "Oh, you're a bit bald there." Some grain was trickled onto the floor and Vera, released from knee-sitting, ate enthusiastically. Then she decided to investigate a work surface, took off

147

like a helicopter, and landed in the middle of the tray with the tea things, upending a sugar bowl and milk container as she skidded to a halt, ending up between the tray and a computer keyboard. The tiny tidal wave of sugary milk that she'd created slopped back and forth in the tray but fortunately didn't make contact with anything electronic.

My first thought was that this would make a good picture, and I started fumbling for my camera, but James, understandably seeing the potential for further disaster, quickly pounced on Vera, and removed her from the table.

An exchange of apologies and "don't worries" ensued, Vera was returned to her cat box, and it seemed a good time for us to start traveling home.

Later, I wondered how to avoid writing an extended plug for some well-to-do ex-design students and their very expensive plastic henhouse (about $550 with chickens), especially since I would be too stingy to buy one, although I could see that, for keeping ill or broody birds, one of these things could work very well.

What I found made life easier. These people were sickeningly nice and talented, had shown a lot of business acumen, and turned an apparently loony idea into a commercially viable thing you could actually buy. They could have been insufferably smug, but weren't.

Later Jane asked to see the pictures of Vera in an Eglu. Naturally, I had forgotten to take any.

11

Beyond the Fringe

BIG IAN DREAMS OF TOAST

"Would you like fishnets and boots?"

It wasn't an unreasonable question. I'd asked for a giant wooden cartoon chicken to attach to the roof of my car and design features needed to be discussed.

If you live on the Isle of Wight you might be familiar with "Big" Ian Gardner, aka "Chawncey" Gardner, aka Chester Longman. He might have fixed your roof, installed your staircase, or done something clever with your cupboards. He's an artist with jigsaws, chisels, and spirit levels.

Actually, he's an artist, full stop. He dabbles in writing, painting, and music, a little in the Dada-inspired vein of musician Viv Stanshall (although the two aren't to be compared musically). So you might have seen him playing in one of the island's pubs—a shambling, six-foot three-inch guitarist with a twizzling mass of curly hair and a rasping, gargled-with-shrapnel voice, whose muses—and vices—include hand-rolled cigarettes and bottles of Newcastle Brown ale.

Big Ian writes songs about fireplace theft, making galleons out of old shopping carts and sailing them over the overpass, vengeful scaffolders, and a family from Surbiton who turn into fish. He does this in a style best described as a musical collision between Led Zeppelin, the Waterboys, and the late comedian Peter Cook. This is a man who wrote a lyric that went,

He's building a rocket
One day he says he'll get to the moon
Got his maths all wrong
And his bollocks shot across the room.

Big Ian was building a conservatory for a friend of mine when I first met him.

"We've had this conversation," said my friend. "Ian was having a cup of tea when he said, 'I'm a bit worried about my brain. I keep having these dreams.'"

"What dreams?" she asked him.

"Oh, you know the sort of thing," said Ian in a matter-of-fact tone, "fields of toast, flying hot-water bottles."

All this might imply that Ian has gone around the bend. He hasn't, but he does operate in a personal, parallel universe, and I knew this made him the ideal person to make an oversized billboard/chicken needed for our final piece of traveling.

Tracking Ian down is never easy. You leave messages on his cell phone, and after a while he responds with cryptic text messages; for instance,

> *'Tis better 2 suffer the slings&arrows of outrageous texting than to be caught frotting with much frivolity&gay abandon into the custard bucket.*

Then the phone rings and you're on a conversational roller coaster that rarely lasts less than an hour, where sticking to the subject is virtually impossible as Ian's firework mind spits out jokes, anecdotes, and thoughts. It's always entertaining and always exhausting.

He liked the idea of the wooden hen.

"How big d'you want the chicken? You want it on the car's roof? What do you think of a chicken with teeth? I could make it look like it's sitting on the toilet."

We decided against the toilet motif, but felt a pair of enormous boots and the fishnet tights ought to be part of the end result. Ian also decided to go for a sort of cutout hen design, three-foot broad by two-foot tall, that could be attached by plastic ties to my car's roof rack.

ON THE FRINGE

This was the "how," but it brought up the "why." Why did I want a huge wooden cartoon chicken stuck on top of my car? The answer was the Edinburgh Fringe, one of the largest arts festivals in the world. The idea was to more or less gatecrash it with both a live chicken and Big Ian's timber-and-paint effort to advertise our presence.

The original plan had been to try signing up for the official event, but several factors got in the way of this. I'd missed the deadline for the program; they wanted a $550 entry fee, plus a percentage of ticket sales; and I'd have to find and pay for a venue. This would have turned a crazy idea into a financially suicidal one, but it still appealed as something to try.

So, some cheating was called for. When our previous road trips were being arranged, Ottakar's branch on George Street in Edinburgh had asked if we wanted to visit them. It seemed a very long way, so we demurred. Would they have us back if some telephone groveling was engaged in? Yes, they said, we were still welcome and they had a slot right at the very end of the Fringe on 27 August.

This was organizationally tight, since on 24 August I would be coming back from a long-planned trip to South America, which meant forty-eight hours to prepare, then drive from Kent to Scotland.

To keep abreast of Big Ian's chicken-making activities, I'd taken my cell phone, but not the charger, and had forgotten to give it an electrical pick-me-up beforehand, so the battery keeled over somewhere near La Paz. Of course, I hadn't written down Ian's cell number since it's stored in my bloody phone. So, I couldn't tell him when we were planning to collect his chicken, or discover whether he'd finished it, or whether he would be staying with family in London, something he'd hoped to be doing when we staggered off the plane at Heathrow—but, since his existence is a bit itinerant, this couldn't be guaranteed.

However, it wasn't Heathrow where Jane and I finally touched English soil again. British Airways was busy having an industrial relations conflict with some of its staff, resulting in our spending twelve hours at the Madrid airport thanks to a canceled connecting flight. It looked as if this could turn into an overnight delay—threatening my ability to get to Edinburgh at all—but, after hours of standing in line with lots of other exhausted, unwashed, and increasingly psychotic travelers, we were told BA might squeeze us onto a Manchester flight. Then Birmingham was mentioned, and we fell upon this offer like rats tearing into a bin liner.

Eighteen hours after we were supposed to have arrived in Britain, we retrieved our car and rolled up outside the home of Big Ian's parents, half expecting it to be empty; but no, a light was on, and when I rang the bell I could see a familiar, loping figure in the opaque glass of the front door.

"Mart! Fuckin' hell. I wondered where you'd got to. Been leaving messages and everything—come and have a look at this!"

Propped up against the kitchen table was a wooden chicken like no other. Half drag queen, half seafront-Saturday-night headbanger, it sported a beak that was curled into a snarl, and featured the promised teeth. Its booted feet were striding as if the thing were out looking for someone to headbutt in a seedy pub.

It was both funny and sinister. Perfect. Afterwards I realized that there were no fishnet tights, but this was more than made up for by the bird's painted earring and very fetching dagger tattoo.

Ian had rigged up a clever hinged attachment arrangement with a plank of two-by-four-foot timber, and showed me how it could be secured to the roof bars of my car, using a fistful of plastic ratchet clips he'd bought for the purpose.

"'Ere. Send us some photographs from Edinburgh will you?" he asked.

THE LATE MR. GURDON

Groggy with jet lag, I spent the following morning cobbling together some posters and flyers, half of which had a painfully obvious spelling mistake. I was too shattered and time was too short to do anything about this, so I mixed them together with the typo-free versions and hoped nobody would notice.

A few days before setting off for South America I'd spoken to the bookshop to discover that they'd had zero interest. "Perhaps it's the entry price. We're charging two dollars to see you." We decided that not charging anything might help, and when I called back was told that they'd had about ten bookings—better than nothing.

It was 2 P.M. the following day when Vera and I set off for Scotland. We'd packed Big Ian's bird, food and sustenance for its real-life companion, a bag of clothes and directions for an eye-wateringly

154

expensive bed-and-breakfast, booked at the last moment, and chosen because it was about the only place left that wasn't full of Fringe-goers. I'd told the proprietor that we'd arrive at 7:30 that evening.

All of sixty miles into the journey I was fighting sleep and had to pull off the highway, trundle along the backroad until I found a suitable rest stop, where I then slept for half an hour, lulled by Vera's shuffling about and clucking to herself in the cat box. Over the next ten and a half hours the journey was punctuated with similar stops, coupled with apologetic phone calls to the B&B as my ETA stretched ever further away.

Night was closing in by the time we were hurtling along the motorway near Teebay in Cumbria. This was when the rain arrived, turning the surface of the road into a very shallow river, with the oc-casional slightly less shallow lake wherever there was a fractional dip in the surface. At this point the car I was driving, a fifteen-year-old BMW station wagon with worn shock absorbers and big fat tires, de-cided to enliven proceedings by impersonating a giant Teutonic pond skater. The technical term for this is "hydroplaning," during which a film of water builds up between tires and road and the car slides along it, perhaps fishtailing in an exciting manner or, for a real laugh, sliding or pirouetting madly until it hits something solid—such as a truck.

Fortunately, Vera and I only got the fishtailing. This meant adopt-ing a trundling pace, grinding along at fifty to sixty miles per hour as the wipers flailed madly, and as I worked on not clutching the steer-ing wheel too hard and tried to relax the muscles that had caused my derrière to clench so that it felt as if my head were brushing the car roof. Sitting quietly in her travel box, Vera seemed entirely unmoved by all of this.

Perhaps it was this frisson that caused me to take the wrong turn to Edinburgh, and instead of finishing the journey on a lit motorway I crept down dark, rain-lashed back roads, which during the day are

recommended by guidebooks as ideal ways to enjoy spectacular Scottish scenery. For me, these wormlike, twisting arteries had lost their charm.

Five miles from the city the slow-moving caravan of cars we'd been part of came to a steaming, drenched halt. Ahead was a big white Mercedes panel van with a tin-opened gash down its side, at one end of which the cause, a new-looking Skoda sedan, was embedded.

By now I'd covered Vera's travel case with a thick, dark coat, and she appeared to be sleeping as I finally reached Edinburgh and proceeded to get lost again. I finally pulled into the B&B parking lot at 12:30 A.M. As I staggered into the hallway the owner insisted that he wasn't put out at having to wait five and a half hours. "At least you phoned," he said.

I'd reached that state of tiredness when your exhausted brain won't switch off. It was pushing 2 A.M. when sleep finally came. I woke five hours later in a fuzz of fatigue to see fingers of sunshine sliding under the curtains. The weather looked promising in a way I wouldn't have dared hope for when doing a motorized breaststroke up the highway.

Vera certainly looked brighter than I did, and as she ate I began the process of lashing Big Ian's bird/beast to my car. Would it fit? He hadn't been able to use my old junker as a template, and I hadn't tried it out before setting off, but had brought a trunk full of tools to hack it about if required. Fortunately, the BMW's roof was just long enough to accommodate it. The thing towered and glowered over Vera and me, and, aware of just how ostentatious it was, I couldn't make up my mind whether to laugh or feel horribly self-conscious.

"You didn't drive up with that on the roof of your car?"

It was the B&B owner, emerging from a side door and apparently convinced that his late night had been caused by a madman driving through a rainstorm while trying to batter the crosswinds out of the way with an outsized wooden chicken.

En route to George Street I got lost again and, despite buying a map, had to stop and ask directions. This resulted in some fabulous, up-and-down eye-swiveling double takes, as people drank in the chicken and then focused their attentions on the guy who'd brought it and whatever was in the cat box next to him.

Questions about this weird ensemble were avoided in a pointed "If I tell him where to go, he'll go away more quickly" kind of way.

George Street itself was a wide, Georgian thoroughfare bathed in sunshine, with parking places in the middle, the inevitable parking meters, and swarms of traffic cops.

I parked, extracted Vera, and, after introducing her to the bookshop staff, asked if there was a back office where she could spend the day. This turned out to be a pleasantly cool office at the top of a worn-looking stone spiral staircase. During the course of the day I made several trips to visit the bird, who seemed to have taken to Edinburgh life, clucking enthusiastically and making "I might lay an egg" noises.

Thanks to preening and scratching-about activities, a crescent of sawdust and claw-shredded newspaper had begun to form outside her carry case, but nobody seemed to mind.

"She's been talking to us," said the manager.

As the morning progressed the weather improved. The sun shone and windows were opened, including those of Vera's office, which was probably just as well for the well-being of its human occupants' noses.

AS THE MONGOOSE SAID TO THE HURRICANE . . .

Out on the street Big Ian's chicken was attracting lots of interest. I'd pasted the car's windows with posters, and managed to wedge a secondhand plastic leaflet holder between a side window and a door frame. Into this I'd stuffed some flyers, and had also taken a deep breath and started to try handing these out too.

157

At one point I'd done something similar for Ian when he was having a serious crack at getting a live audience in London for his music. He was mostly playing pub venues on wet Tuesday nights, but secured a one-time warm-up slot for an Irish band called the Saw Doctors, who were playing a big venue called the Clapham Grand. The place was packed, and I spent most of the evening squeezing in among a surging crowd and handing out flyers on where Ian was playing next: a toilet-sized back room at the Mean Fiddler in Harlesden.

Doing this for somebody else is far easier than handing out bits of paper that promote yourself. An English terror of being in other people's faces made the process in Edinburgh a toe-curling one. "Er, hello. I'm a journalist with a chicken. Would you mind terribly missing all the professional entertainment on offer at the moment and coming to see us? Um, it's free."

I did have the advantage of being parked just across the road from the Assembly Rooms theater, a venue running a box office for a va-

riety of events. Long lines of ticket buyers formed regularly, and, unlike people walking along the street, they couldn't escape so easily. This meant leaflet distributors buzzed around them like flies.

I decided that honesty was probably the best policy. "Would you like some wastepaper to go with the other wastepaper?"

Only a few people said no.

Weaving in and out of the line, I worked from the far end to the front, meeting the other leaflet distributors coming the other way and swapping flyers with most of them. Potential rivals for Vera and me included a play called *Mongoose* ("the story of Ted, trying to come to terms with the death of his lifelong friend, a talking mongoose") and *Kenneth—What Is The Frequency?*, a play featuring a talking hurricane.

ENTER SIR JOHN, STAGE LEFT

Every so often I'd have to move the car to another parking spot and spoon-feed the parking meters to avoid traffic-cop terror.

By mid-afternoon I'd finished the latest round of flyer mugging and was on my way to find a sandwich and a pet shop—Vera needed fresh sawdust—when a cultured voice said, "Hello. John Gielgud."

Standing in front of me was a tall, patrician man with a cravat. He sounded very like Gielgud, but being quick off the mark I knew at once this wasn't really the theatrical knight, who would have been one hundred years old had he not died four years previously. I'd also seen the real thing. My dad worked in television and was involved in an Agatha Christie show in which Gielgud was the star. I was about thirteen and told to stand very still on the fringe of the set and to *not move*. During a scene change the great man stood not quite in the middle of the studio until a plump armchair was procured. He then sat, casting a brief, severe glance in my direction before staring into the middle distance as cast, crew, and large chunks of set were rearranged around him.

The fake Sir John spoke again. "Would you like this?" A flyer promoting a one-man show called *Gielgud—A Knight in the Theater*, starring an actor called George Telfer, was gently proffered.

"Here, have one of mine," I said, digging out a limp, homemade job with a spelling mistake.

"Thank you so much."

I asked if his feet were aching yet. "Oh, yes," he said, remaining in softly fruity-voiced character. "I've been doing this all day."

We wished each other luck.

I found the pet shop at what seemed to be the outer edge of the city, bought the sawdust, and asked if they'd take some flyers for something that was, after all, animal-related.

"Is that all you've got? I could do wi' a few more," said the fierce-looking woman behind the counter.

I had only a few left—fresh supplies were back at the car, and I was surprised by the interest.

"We get lots of Fringe people coming in and buying tartan dog collars to wear," said the woman in a tone of voice that indicated I was a bit slow on the uptake.

Later I went back to the shop in the car to provide them with a fresh supply of flyers, then ground my way up Princes Street so that the populace at large could get the full benefit of Ian's chicken, which attracted a steady stream of gawkers. At one point a woman in a taxi, who could have had the word "tourist" embossed on her forehead, dug out a camera and started taking pictures.

Children were particularly taken by the creature. Small fingers pointed, high-pitched voices squeaked and laughed. The sun was blazing, and as I'd opened the sunroof and windows I could hear every cackle. At a traffic light an elegant dad did his best to tow a small child of about five rapidly across the road, but his plans were not helped by Big Ian's creation.

"Look! Chicken!" said the child.

"Ye-es," said Daddy, in a not quite approving tone. "It looks like a very aggressive chicken to me."

In between these forays I sneaked into places such as Starbucks (hmmm, love their coffee—no, really, I wouldn't lie about a thing like that) to secrete little piles of flyers. I even tried the local tourist office, but made the mistake of asking. "No, thank you," said a steely-eyed girl. "We don't have enough space."

As the hours drifted by, the process of handing out those bisected bits of paper grew harder and harder. It seemed such a bloody imposition on people who were just minding their own business.

"Would you like some more wastepaper?"

I knew it was time to give up when I'd offloaded about 400 flyers and had spent about twenty minutes not giving out the remaining fifty or sixty. The time had come to stop wandering about. Back I trudged to the car, dumped the remainder of the flyers in the plastic dispenser, and went in search of a cup of tea, feeling worn out and mentally underpowered.

ENTER VERA, STAGE RIGHT

About twenty people came to see Vera and me that evening, including three very old ladies, who I suspect were serial book-signing attendees. "When does the man start his talk?" asked the tiniest citizen five minutes after they'd arrived and swooped on the complimentary drinks. "Och, another ten minutes. Time for another glass of wine, I think!" Walking sticks flailing, they moved quickly to liberate further glasses of red. Somebody mentioned afterwards that this pensionable trio usually had a fourth, equally venerable, friend in tow who "likes asking inappropriate questions." I was rather sad to have missed her.

Vera dealt with the subsequent attention like the seasoned pro she had become. I felt more exhausted than ever and talked reheated,

161

warmed-over gibberish, but nobody noticed. And, yes, I was asked if we ate our chickens.

Later, with Vera tucked up in her travel box, I dined alone in a fish-and-chips restaurant and considered the day's events.

A hideous, 500-mile drive, a roof-mounted wooden chicken, and a day rattling around the streets of Edinburgh thrusting one-paragraph begging letters into the hands of several hundred people who were trying to mind their own business had achieved what? Nothing. Zilch. Nada. Not one of the people Vera and I saw had turned up thanks to these efforts. They'd all prebooked, and would have come to see us—or those lovely glasses of wine—if I'd had a good nap at the B&B, then spent the rest of the day sightseeing.

At least the Fringe professionals, who'd paid their dues here—financially and professionally—hadn't lost out thanks to our turning up.

On a personal level it didn't matter. Almost a year before, when the traveling chicken odyssey that brought us here first got under way, I had no conception of the geographical and personal twists and turns it would involve.

Now it was almost over. I hadn't learned anything about hens that a trip to the bottom of the garden wouldn't offer up, but the journey had provided some superb people-watching opportunities. Encounter your fellow human beings with a domestic fowl as a sidekick and they're likely to be taken off guard, surprised, and intrigued. Since, generally speaking, it isn't you they're interested in, it's possible to be both at the center of things and an observer. What more could a writer ask for?

As for the process of writing, I didn't guess that it would offer a peculiar sustaining quality when it was time to say good-bye to old friends, or that writing about them in the context of the journey would start the process of being liberated from their loss. To describe this as "cathartic" is almost a cliché, but such things often become clichés because they're true.

I had suspected that traveling with a chicken would bring me into contact with new people, some of whom might in time become friends too, and expose me to events and places I would otherwise have missed, and so it proved.

Whatever; by the time Vera and I reached Edinburgh, I'd already spent weeks engaged in the professional equivalent of contemplating my navel. Why had I done it? Fun. The whole thing had been a blast. No other reason was needed. I drank some lukewarm tea and felt happy.

Memories, apparently, are made of this—the "this" in question being weeks spent zinging from one part of the country to another with a chicken in a plastic box. The next journey would be our last, the one that took us home. Had she known, I suspected that the box's current occupant would have looked forward to it as much as I did.